百年总统府

The Hundred-Year History of the Presidential Palace

主编　刘晓宁　郭必强

Chief Editor　Liu Xiaoning　Guo Biqiang

南京出版传媒集团 南京出版社

Nanjing Publishing House

策　　划　卢海鸣　樊立文

主　　编　刘晓宁　郭必强

编　　辑（以姓氏笔画为序）

王培智　叶永坚　刘重光　李　宁　吴小宝

吴志斌　陈宝珠　夏　彪　喻春生　管　辉

英文翻译　孙修福

图文统筹　肖　木　徐　智

技术支持　高旭青　任维波

摄　　影　沈　旻　陈宁骏

目 录

前 言

总统府，位于今南京长江路，是中国规模最大、保存最为完好的近代历史建筑群。史上曾有四次使用总统府名称。

总统府遗址，明朝为汉王府，清朝为两江总督署。1853年3月19日，太平天国军队攻占南京，改称天京，定为都城。洪秀全自封天王，割据一方，与清王朝分庭抗礼，并在清两江总督署原址大兴土木，开始建造规模宏大的天朝宫殿（天王府）。经数年的营造，太平天国天王府已是方圆数里，殿阙巍峨，金碧辉煌。1864年7月19日，清军攻破天京，焚烧天朝宫殿。只可惜，“十年壮丽天王府，化作荒庄野鸽飞”，仅存一座石舫。之后，曾国藩在天王府的废墟上重建两江总督署，沿袭了原总督署的规模和规制，修建了大门、东西辕门、照壁以及大堂、二堂等建筑，并复建了东、西花园，基本形成了今天的建筑格局。

1911年10月，辛亥革命爆发。12月2日，江浙联军光复南京。12月29日，已独立的十七省代表选举孙中山为中华民国临时大总统。

1912年1月1日，孙中山在原清两江总督署宣誓就任中华民国临时大总统，并组建了中华民国临时政府。这里成为中国历史上第一个共和国的总统府所在地。孙中山以革命为己任，立志救国救民，在这里进行了一系列伟大的变革。孙中山先生是伟大的民族英雄、伟大的爱国主义者、中国民主革命的伟大先驱，为中华民族做出了彪炳史册的贡献。孙大总统的办公室，就设在西花园的西花厅。1912年4月3日，孙中山践诺解职离开了总统府。

之后，北洋政府在此设立留守府，以黄兴为留守。数月后仍改为都督府，程德全为都督。1913年6月，黄兴发起讨袁之役，在此设立讨袁军总司令部，结果兵败。何海鸣自封讨袁军临时总司令，三度占领都督府。9月1日，辫帅张勋攻入南京，剿灭讨袁军，复称都督府，自称江苏都督。在以后的十多年中，都督府中各路豪强纷纷在此登场角逐，政权的更迭极为频繁。这里先后成为江苏将军府、江苏督军署、中华民国副总统府、江苏督办公署、江苏宣抚使署、苏浙皖赣闽五省联军总司令部、直鲁联军联合办事处等。

1927年3月23日，北伐军攻克南京，以原督军署为国民革命军和北伐军总司令部。4

月18日，国民政府成立，以南京为首都，在原临时参议院办公。9月，国民政府迁至整修后的原督军署。1928年10月，国民政府实行“五院制”，辟国府东院为行政院，国府西院为国民政府参谋本部和主计处。

1932年1月28日，淞沪战争爆发，1月31日，国民政府被迫移驻洛阳。同年12月迁回南京。1937年七七事变后，日军兵临南京。11月16日，国民政府迁都重庆。

1937年12月，南京沦陷。国民政府被日军第16师团占为本部驻地。1938年3月，伪维新政府在此成立。1940年3月，汪精卫的伪国府成立后，在此设立了监察院、立法院、考试院，国府东院（原行政院）则为交通部和铁道部。

1946年5月，国民政府从重庆“还都”南京，仍以此为国民政府。国府东院辟为社会部、地政部、水利部和侨务委员会，西花园则先后作为国民政府军令部和首都卫戍总司令部等。

1948年4月，在“行宪”国大上，蒋介石、李宗仁分别当选“总统”“副总统”，5月就任。国民政府则改称总统府。

1949年1月21日，蒋介石下野，由李宗仁代理“总统”，仍以此为总统府。

1949年4月23日，南京解放。4月24日凌晨，人民解放军占领总统府。从此，总统府跨入新纪元。

百年总统府，弹指一挥间。总统府作为一个时代终结的重要坐标和新时代的开端，它经历了辉煌，也蒙受过耻辱，它是中国近代史的一个缩影，也是一部历史教科书。重视历史，研究历史，借鉴历史，可以给我们带来很多了解昨天、把握今天、开创明天的智慧。承载百年历史风云的总统府，现已成为海内外瞩目的中国近代史遗址博物馆。今天，中国比历史上任何时期都更接近中华民族伟大复兴的目标。以百年总统府为历史背景，集中展示近代中国历史进程与这座世界著名历史建筑群的风雨沧桑，可以促进海峡两岸同胞交流和交往，完成祖国统一大业，激励人们为实现中华民族伟大复兴的中国梦而努力奋斗。

Introduction

The Presidential Palace is located at Changjiang Road in Nanjing. It is the largest scale and the most properly protected architectural complex of modern Chinese history. It had been named "Presidential Palace" four times in different times during the republican period.

The former site of the Presidential Palace was the "Prince Han's" Residence in the Ming Dynasty and the Liangjiang Viceroy's Official Residence in the Qing Dynasty.

On 19 March 1853, the Taiping Troops occupied Jiangning (Nanjing).The Taiping Heavenly Kingdom made Jiangning the capital and renamed it as Tianjing (Heavenly Capital). Hong Xiuquan who proclaimed himself as Heavenly King, erected Heavenly Dynasty Palace (also called Heavenly King's Residence) in the compound of the former Liangjiang Viceroy's Official Residence. It was extremety ornate and magnificent.Manchu Troops recovered Tianjing and burnt down the Heavenly Dynasty Palace on 19 July 1864.Unfortunately, the majestic view of ten-year-heavenly king's residence was destroyed in a moment. After that, Zeng Guofan, Liangjiang Viceroy, rebuilt Liangjiang Viceroy's Official Residence on the ruins of the Heavenly King's Residence. The scale and structure of the reconstructed Liangjiang Viceroy's Official Residence were patterned to the former one. The East and West Gardens were also restored. It had formed the basic building structure as seen today.

In October 1911, the 1911 Revolution broke out. The Jiang (su) -Zhe (jiang) Allied Army recaptured Nanjing on 2 December. The 17 newly independent provinces elected Dr. Sun Yat-sen as Provisional President of the Republic of China on 29 December. On 1 January 1912, Dr. Sun Yat-sen took his oath of office, and found the first republican government—the Provisional Government of the Republic of China in Chinese history in the former Liangjiang Viceroy's Official Residence. More than two thousand years of feudalism in China came to an end. Dr. Sun Yat-sen took revolution as his mission and determined to save the nation and the people. He made a series of great changes during his term of office. Dr Sun Yat-sen was a great national hero, a great patriot and a great pioneer of China's democratic revolution, and made great contributions to the history of the Chinese nation. President Sun Yat-sen's Office was located in the West Follower Hall of the West Garden of the Liangjiang Viceroy's Official Residence.

Dr. Sun Yat-sen carried out his promise to resign from his Provisional Presidency and left the Presidential Palace on 3 April 1912. After that, the Beiyang Government set up Nanjing Resident-General's Office and appointed Huang Xing as Nanjing Resident-General. Several months later, the Resident-General's Office was abolished. The Jiangsu Military Governor's Office was restored, with Cheng Dequan as the Governor.

In June 1913, Huang Xing launched an Anti-Yuan (Shih-kai) battle and set up the Headquarters of the Jiangsu Anti-Yuan Army here. Unfortunately, he failed. He Haimin proclaimed himself Provisional Commander-in-Chief of the Anti-Yuan Army and occupied the Jiangsu Military Governor's Office three times as his headquarters. Zhang Xun's "Pigtail Troops" occupied Nanjing on 1 September and proclaimed himself Jiangsu Military Governor.

In the following decades, warlords fought against one another for the control of Nanjing, and regimes changed frequently. Here successively became the Jiangsu Military Governor's Official Residence; the Jiangsu General's Official Residence; the Office of the Jiangsu Pacification Commission; the Headquarters of the Five-Province Allied Troops; the Joint Office of Zhili-Shandong Allied Forces. Feng Guozhang also set his Vice Presidential Office of the Beiyang Warlords Government here.

The Northern Expeditionary Army occupied Nanjing on 23 March 1927. The Headquarters of the National Revolutionary Army and the Northern Expeditionary Army was set up in the former Jiangsu Military Governor's Official Residence.

The Nationalist Government was established on 18 April 1927 and made Nanjing its capital. The Government occupied the former Jiangsu Provincial Assembly before they moved to the former Jiangsu Military Governor's Official Residence in September 1927.

The Nationalist Government was reformed into "Five-Yuan" in October 1928. The Executive Yuan used the east courtyard of the Government as its seats. The Headquarters of the General Staff and the Comptroller-General's Office occupied a part of the West Garden.

Following the outbreak of the Song-Hu Anti-Japanese Campaign on 28 January 1932, the Nationalist Government moved its capital to Luoyang, Henan Province on 31 January 1932 and returned to Nanjing in December of the same year. After the outbreak of the 1937 Lugouqiao (Marco Polo Bridge) Incident, as the Japanese troops moved closer to Nanjing, the Nationalist Government moved its capital to Chongqing, Sichuan Province on 16 November 1937.

Nanjing was occupied by Japanese troops in December 1937. They took over the compound of the Nationalist Government as headquarters for the 16th Division of the Japanese Imperial Army.

The Executive Yuan of the so-called "Reformed Government" used the compound as their seats in March 1938. After the establishment of Wang Jingwei's Puppet government in March 1940, the compound served as the offices of the Control Yuan, Legislative Yuan, Examination Yuan, Ministries of Communications and Railways.

In May 1946, the Nationalist Government returned to Nanjing from Chongqing. It and its subordinates units such as Ministries of Social Affairs, Land Administration and Conservancy, Overseas Chinese Affairs Commission used east garden as premise; the Ministry of Military Affairs and Headquarters of Capital Garrison, moved their offices back the compound of west garden of the Nationalist Government.

Chiang Kai-shek was elected President of the Republic of China on 18 April and Li Zongren was elected Vice President on 29 April 1949, the Nationalist Government was thus renamed the Presidential Government in May 1949.

On 21 January 1949, Chiang Kai-shek decided to "temporarily retire from office", Li Zongren then held the office of Acting President.

On 23 April 1949, Nanjing was liberated. In the early morning of 24 April, the People's Liberation Army occupied the Presidential Palace. The Kuomintang's rule in mainland China came to an end. From this day onwards, the Presidential Palace has strode into a new era.

As an important mark for the end of an era and the beginning of a new era, the Presidential Palace has experienced magnificence and humiliation. It is a miniature of China's modern history and a history textbook. Paying attention to history, studying history and learning from it can bring us a lot of wisdom to understand yesterday, grasp today and create tomorrow. Through all the ups and downs in the world for more than 100 years, the Presidential Palace has become the Nanjing Historic Relics Museum of Modern Chinese History which attracted worldwide attention. Today China is closer than at any time in history to the goal of the great rejuvenation of the Chinese nation. Taking the Presidential Palace as the historical background and focusing on the historical process of modern China and the vicissitudes of this world-renowned historical complex, it can promote the exchanges and exchanges between compatriots on both sides of the Taiwan Straits, accomplish the reunification of the motherland, and inspire people to work hard to realize the Chinese dream of the great rejuvenation of the Chinese nation.

一

太平军兴　十年壮丽天王府

I. Taiping Troops Uprising　Majestic View of Ten-Year-Heavenly King's Palace

1853年3月19日，太平军沿长江东下，攻克江宁（今南京），易名天京并定为都城。太平天国在这里进行了一系列反对清王朝的政治、军事、经济活动。天王洪秀全在清朝两江总督署原址兴建了气势巍峨、壮丽辉煌的天朝宫殿（天王府）。1864年7月，清军攻陷天京，天朝宫殿被付之一炬，真是“十年壮丽天王府，化作荒庄野鸽飞”。

On 19 March 1853, the Taiping Troops occupied Jiangning (now Nanjing). The Taiping Heavenly Kingdom made Jiangning its capital and renamed it Tianjing (heavenly capital). The Taiping Heavenly Kingdom undertook a series of political, military and economic activities against the Qing Government. Hong Xiuquan, Heavenly King, erected the Heavenly Dynasty Palace (also called the Heavenly King's Residence) in the compound of the former Liangjiang Viceroy's Official Residence. It was broad in scale and sumptuous with many buildings and pavilions. Qing Troops recovered Tianjing and burnt down the Heavenly Dynasty Palace in July, 1864. Unfortunately, the majestic view of ten-year-Heavenly King's Residence was destroyed in a moment.

天王洪秀全（雕塑）

Statue of Hong Xiuquan, Heavenly King

十年壮丽天王府（模型）

Majestic View of Ten-Year Heavenly King's Residence (A model)

天王旨准玺拓本

Rubbings from Heavenly King's Seal "Memorial Granted"

天王玉玺拓本

Words of Heavenly King's Seal

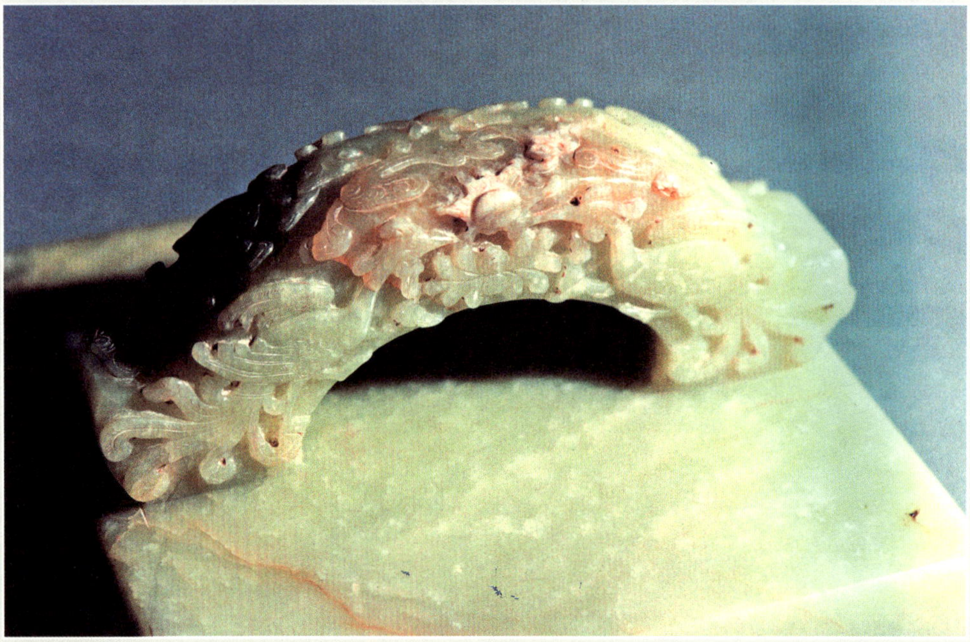

天王玉玺

Heavenly King's Seal

英国人呤唎所著《太平天国革命亲历记》中的洪秀全像

Hong Xiuquan's Portrait in A. F. Lindley's Book: "Ti-Ping Tien Kowh : The History of the Ti-Ping Revolution, Including a Narrative of the Author's Personal Adventures"

太平天国天朝宫殿崇圣殿（英国传教士卡拉摩萨绘制）

Chong Sheng Hall of the Taiping Heavenly Kingdom (drawn by Kara Mossa, Englishman in 1850)

五色井。井栏遇水即呈五色，为天朝宫殿被焚后唯一保存完好的遗迹（2006 年在原国民政府主计处发现）

"Five-colour Well", when its curb with water, it became five colours. It is the sole relic of the Heavenly Dynasty Palace. It was discovered in 2006.

太平天国的“革命纲领”《天朝田亩制度》

Block-printed Edition of “Land System of Heavenly Dynasty”

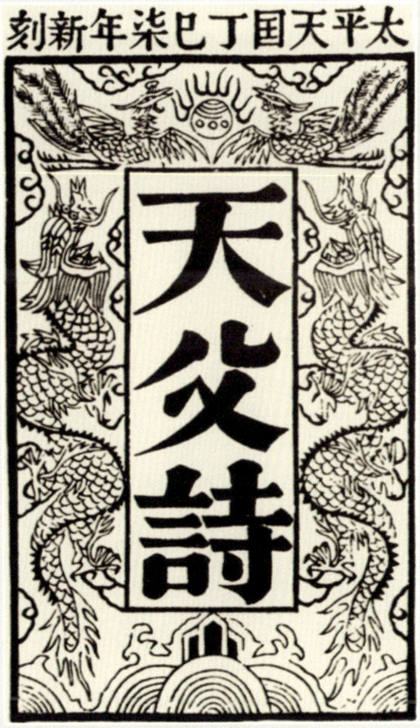

洪秀全著《天父诗》刻本

Block-printed Edition of “Poems of Heavenly Father” Written by Hong Xiuquan

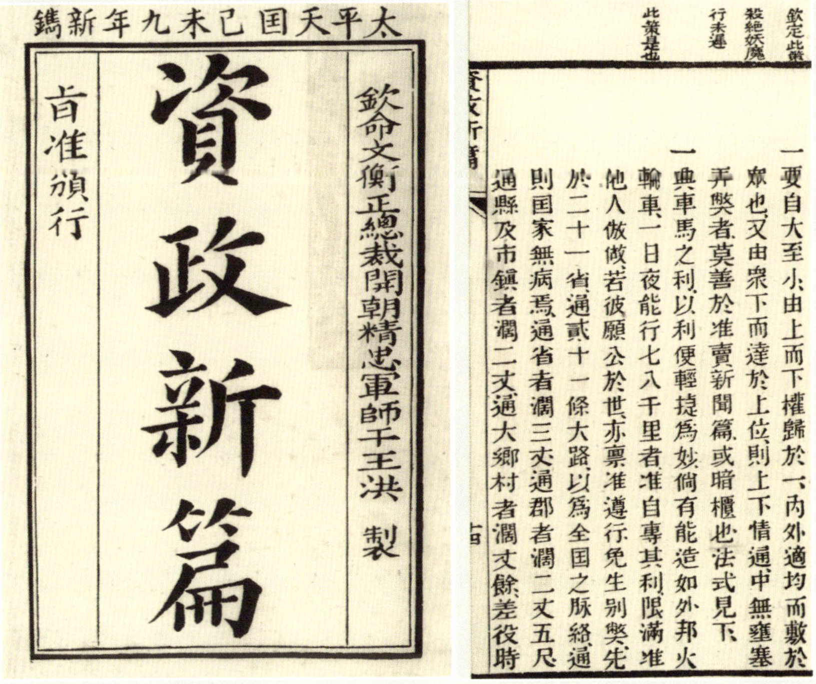

欽定此策
殺絶妖魔
行未遲
此策是也

一要自大至小由上而下權歸於一、內外適均而敷於
衆也、又由衆下而達於上位、則上下情通、中無壅塞
弄弊者、莫善於准賣新聞篇、或暗櫃也、法式見下、
一興車馬之利、以利便輕捷為妙、倘有能造如外邦火
輪車、一日夜能行七八千里者、准自專其利、限滿准
他人倣做、若彼願公於世、亦禀准遵行、免生別弊、先
於二十一省、通貳十一條大路、以為全国之脉絡、通
則国家無病焉、通省者濶三丈、通郡者濶二丈五尺、
通縣及市鎮者濶二丈、通大鄉村者濶丈餘、差役時

《资政新篇》刻本及天王洪秀全批语

Block-printed Edition of “New Policy of Heavenly Dynasty” and Hong Xiuquan’s Comments

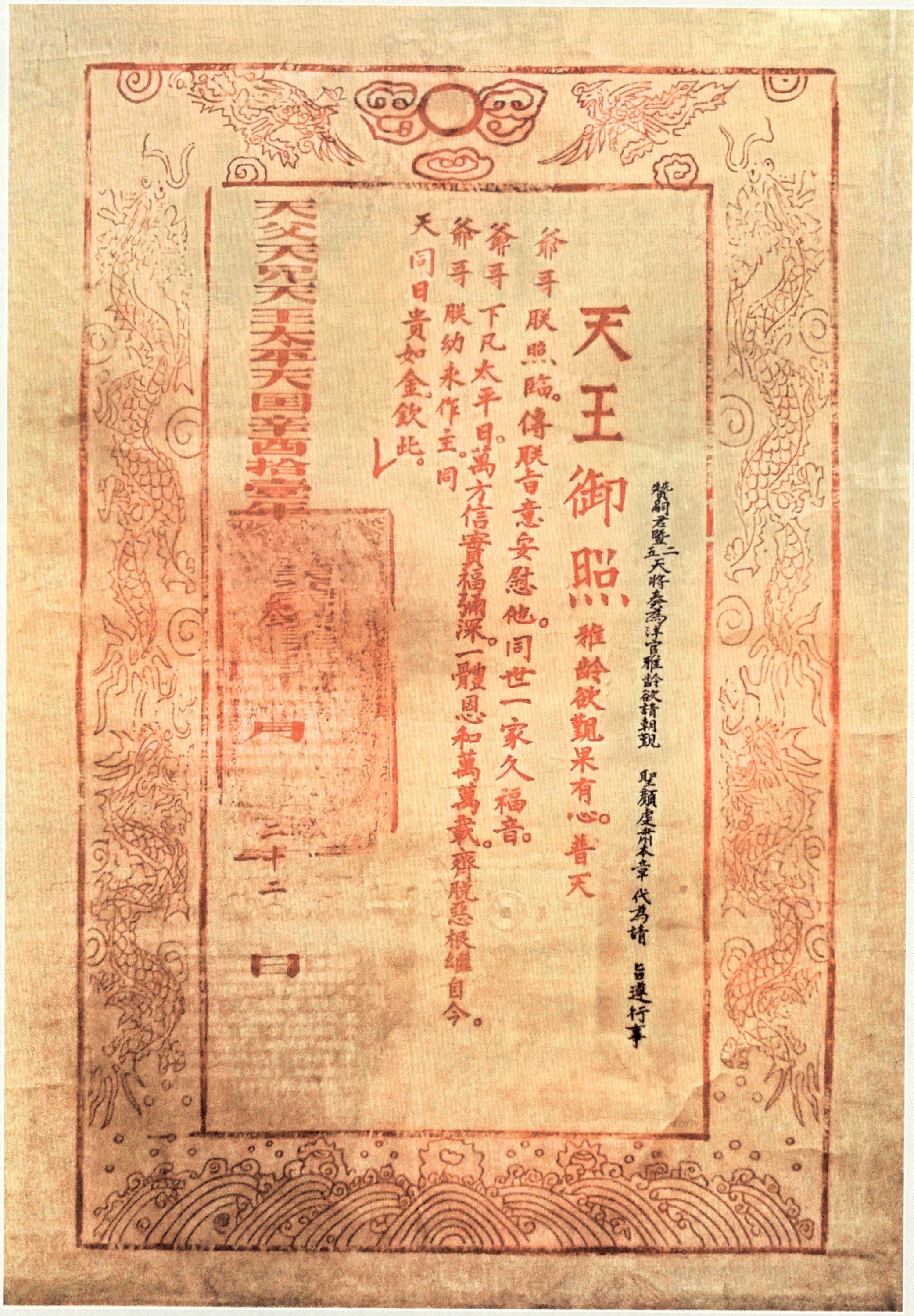

天王御照是太平天国独创的文书体裁。这是1861年5月2日天王洪秀全发给英国“怪物”号舰长雅龄要求觐见的御照

Heavenly King's royal according was created by the Taiping Heavenly Kingdom. It was what Hong Xiuquan issued to the captain of English warship "Monster" on 2 May 1861.

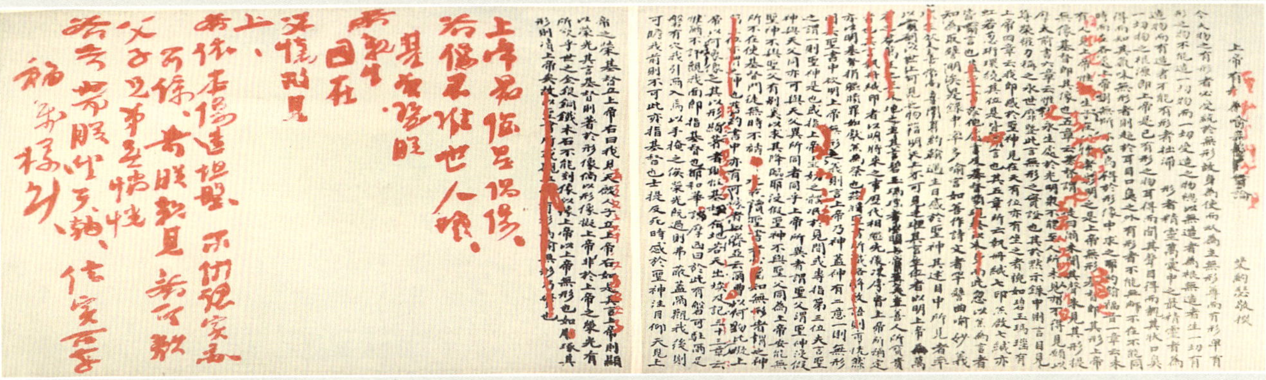

1861 年 3 月，天王洪秀全在英国传教士艾约瑟撰文上的手批

Hong Xiuquan's Written Comments on the Writings of Joseph Edkins, English Churchman in March 1861

天王詔旨

朕詔蘇省及所屬郡縣四民知之
爺哥朕幼坐天京救民塗炭拯民生民
有飢溺
朕飢溺痌瘝在抱秉至情何況爾
民新歸附前遭妖毒陷害深
復經
天兵申
天討遺家棄產
朕憫憐
上帝基督帶
朕幼照見民困發政仁酌減徵收
舒民力期無失所安衆心共
體
爺哥朕幼意咸遵真道樂太平
朕覽秀胞本奏歷述蘇省所屬郡
縣新附四民前經胡妖抽捐
抽稅竭盡爾等脂膏厚斂重
征同
天打門兹經
天朝統率大衆奉行
[illegible]救民水炎之中同中萬郭歸
爺天義勗哉四民既列版圖各宜遵守
條命信定認真克守
天教朕又念前時
天兵征剿爾等四民畏懼
天威拋棄家產今雖欣然就撫各安農
業際此新天新地之期未有
餘一倍三之積
朕格外體邮民艱於爾民應征錢
漕正款今該地佐將酌減若
干爾庶民得薄一分賦稅即
寬出無限生機其各體諒
朕心益堅信認安居樂業同頂
爺哥朕幼綱常同享真福於萬萬年也
欽此
太平天国庚申十年九月二十四日詔

天王诏旨

Heavenly King's Imperial Edicts

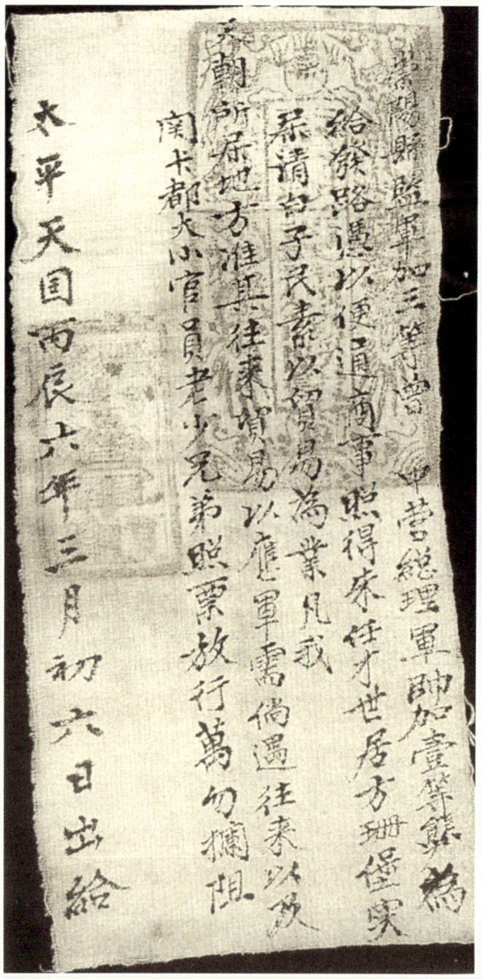

太平天国颁发的路凭（通行证）

Passport Issued by the Taiping Heavenly Kingdom

太平天国腰牌（出入凭证）

Gate Pass Issued by the Taiping Heavenly Kingdom

太平天国翼王石达开部“护封”铜印及印文

Bronze Seal and Seals of Shi Dakai, the Yi Wang of the Taiping Heavenly Kingdom

当时绘制的太平天国妇女像

Woman Portrait in the Taiping Heavenly Kingdom Period

太平天国壁画——云龙图

Dragon and Clouds, Wall Painting of the Taiping Heavenly Kingdom

天朝宫殿侍卫衙《喜临城苑图》（壁画）

Wall Painting "Tianjing City Full of Happiness" in the Imperial Bodyguard Room of the Heavenly Dynasty Palace

太平天国尊崇上帝教。这是太平天国组织举行宗教活动时的场景（英国人呤唎所著《太平天国革命亲历记》中的绘画）

The Taiping Heavenly Kingdom worshiped the God. This picture shows the religious activities by them, in A. F. Lindley's book: "Ti-Ping Tien Kowh".

太平天国诸王穿着的龙袍

Heavenly King's Imperial Robe

太平天国上层官员穿着的团龙褂

Group Dragon Gown Worn by Top Officials of the Taiping Heavenly Kingdom

太平天国使用的清朝钱币

Qing Dynasty Coins Used by the Taiping Heavenly Kingdom

太平天国发行的钱币

Gilded Dragon-phoenix Coins Issued by the Taiping Heavenly Kingdom

太平天国圣库砝码

Weights Used by the State Treasury of the Taiping Heavenly Kingdom

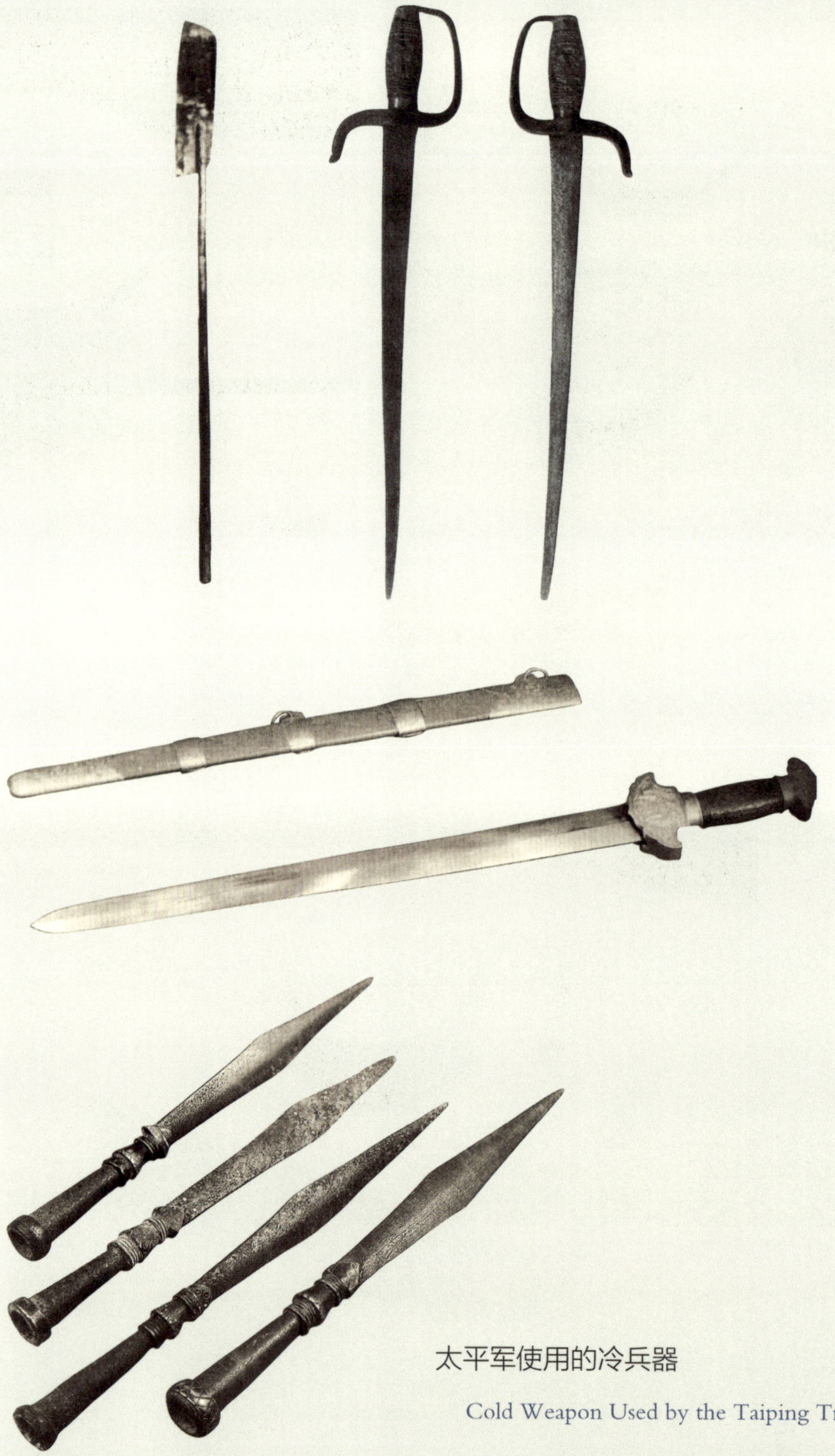

太平军使用的冷兵器

Cold Weapon Used by the Taiping Troops

太平军的装备——洋炮

Guns— Equipment of the Taiping Troops

太平军的装备——铜炮

Bronze Guns— Equipment of the Taiping Troops

太平军的重型装备——前膛炮

Big Gun—Weight Equipment of the Taiping Troops

抬枪

Firearms

太平军防卫兵器——擂石

Rolling Stone—Defense Weapon of the Taiping Troops

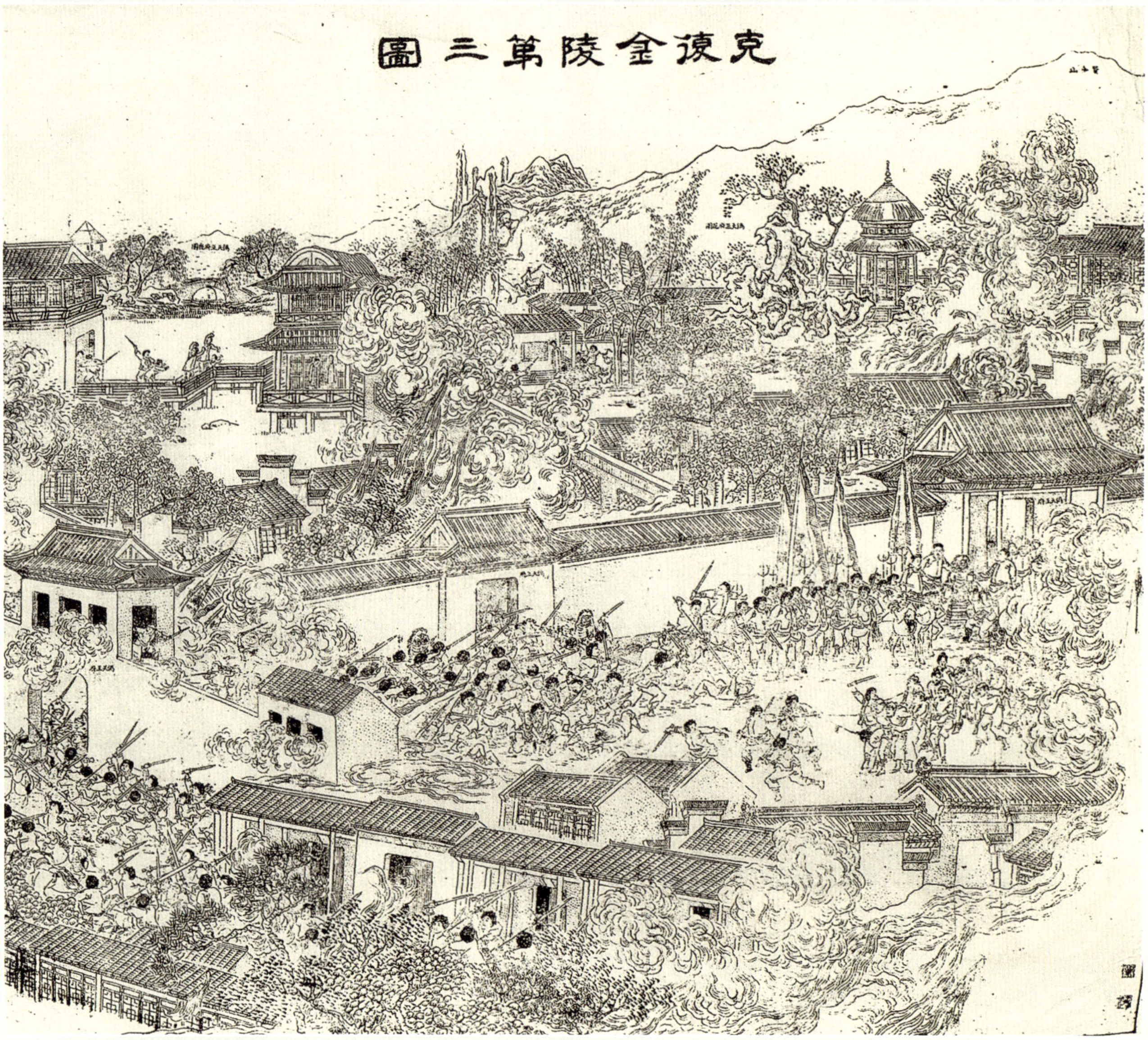

1864 年 7 月 19 日，清军攻陷天京。这是清人彭鸿年绘制的《焚烧天朝宫殿图》

On 19 July 1864, the Qing Troops occupied Tianjing. This picture illustrates the Qing Troops burning the Heavenly Dynasty Palace (drawn by Peng Hongnian in the Qing Dynasty).

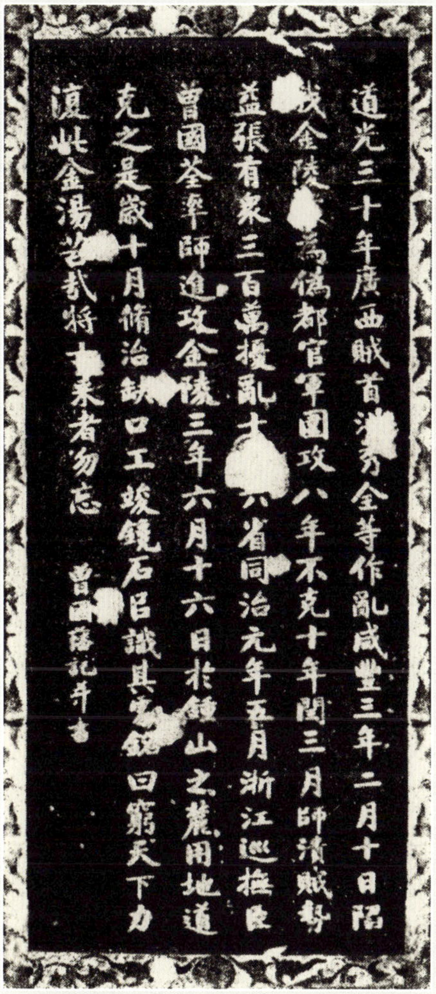

道光三十年廣西賊首洪秀全等作亂咸豐三年二月十日陷
我金陵[illegible]為僞都官軍圍攻八年不克十年閏三月師潰賊勢
益張有衆三百萬擾亂十六省同治元年五月浙江巡撫臣
曾國荃率師進攻金陵三年六月十六日於鍾山之麓用地道
克之是歲十月脩治缺口工竣鑱石記識其處銘曰窮天下力
復此金湯苦哉將士來者勿忘
曾國藩記并書

曾国藩撰写的缺口碑文，记述了湘军攻占天京的情形

Rubbing of An Inscription on the Tablet Written by Zeng Guofan, which described the recapture of Tianjing by the Hunan Forces

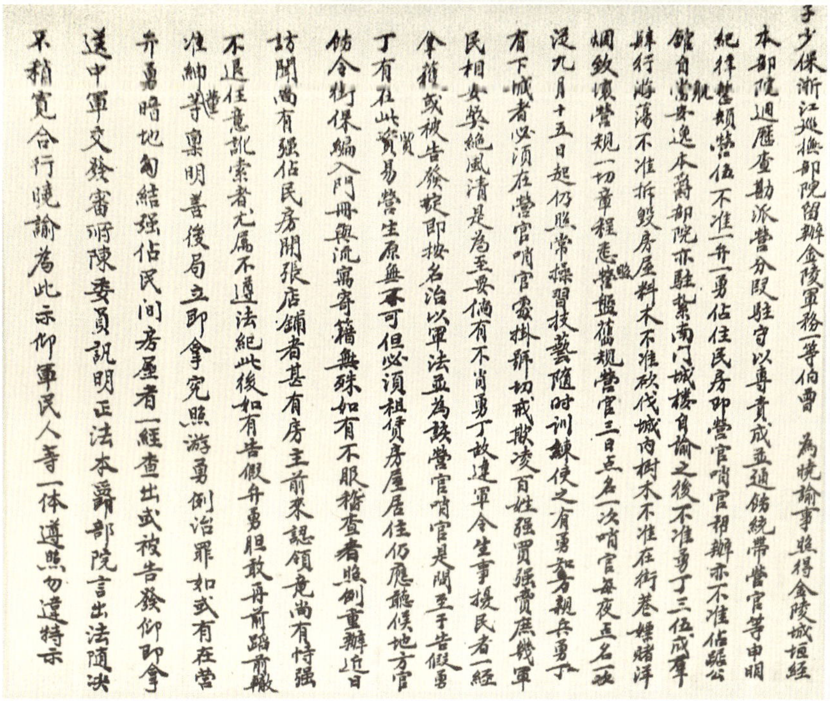

太子少保浙江巡撫部院留辦金陵軍務一等伯曾　為曉諭事照得金陵城垣經
本部院迴歷查勘派營分段駐守以專責成並通飭統帶營官等申明
紀律整頓營伍不准一弁一勇佔住民房即營官哨官幫辦亦不准佔踞公
館自當安逸本爵部院亦駐紮南門城樓自諭之後不准勇丁三伍成羣
肆行游蕩不准拆毀房屋料木不准砍伐城內樹木不准在街巷嫖賭洋
烟致壞營規一切章程悉照舊規營官三日點名一次哨官每夜點名一次
從九月十五日起仍照常操習技藝隨時訓諭使之有勇知方親兵勇丁
有下城者必須在營官哨官處掛號切戒欺凌百姓強買強賣庶幾軍
民相安弊絕風清是為至要倘有不肖勇丁故違軍令生事擾民者一經
拿獲或被告發定即按名治以軍法並為該營官哨官是問至于告假勇
丁有在此貿易營生原無不可但必須租賃房屋居住仍應稟候地方官
飭令街保編入門冊與流寓寄籍無殊如有不服稽查者照例重辦近日
訪聞尚有強佔民房開張店鋪者甚有房主前來認領竟尚有恃強
不退任意訛索者尤屬不遵法紀此後如有告假弁勇膽敢再蹈前轍
准紳董等稟明善後局立即拿究照游勇例治罪如或有在營
弁勇暗地勾結強佔民間房屋者一經查出或被告發仰即拿
送中軍支發審所陳委員訊明正法本爵部院言出法隨決
不稍寬合行曉諭為此示仰軍民人等一體遵照勿違特示

湘军统领曾国荃在攻陷天京后颁发的布告

Notification Issued by Zeng Guoquan, Commander of the Hunan Forces After the Occupation of Tianjing

天朝宫殿石鼓

Stone Drums in the Heavenly Dynasty Palace

天朝宫殿内宫石门档

Door-stones of the Inner Court Gateway of the Heavenly Dynasty Palace

天朝宫殿残存石构件

Stone Structural Supports from the Heavenly Dynasty Palace of the Taiping Heavenly Kingdom

天国风云（油画）

Raging Struggle of the Taiping Heavenly Kingdom (Oil Painting)

二

三省钧衡　两江保障镇江南

II. San Sheng Jun Heng (equilibrium of three provinces) Liangjiang Viceroy Guarding Jiangnan

清朝两江地区即江苏（含上海）、安徽和江西，有“东南锁钥”“财赋重地”之称。两江总督是该地区军政合一的最高长官，始设于康熙四年（1665年），至宣统三年（1911年），历上百任，多为清朝一品、二品官员担任。林则徐、曾国藩、左宗棠、李鸿章、沈葆桢、张之洞等清廷重臣均任过该职。两江总督署位于江宁城中原明汉王府旧址，太平天国后重建。

The area known as Liangjiang in the Qing Dynasty comprised the region of Jiangnan (including the provinces of Jiangsu and Anhui) and Jiangxi provinces. Shanghai was under Jiangsu's jurisdiction at that time. It was " the key of southeastern China" and "the major place of taxes and levies". In the fourth year of the reign of Emperor Kangxi (1865), the Qing Imperial Government began to assign a Liangjiang Viceroy who was the top leader of these three places. There were nearly a hundred men (officials of the first or second rank) who took up the post of it till the end of the Qing Dynasty in 1911. The famous officials among them, such as Lin Zexu, Zeng Guofan, Zuo Zongtang, Li Hongzhang, Shen Baozhen and Zhang Zhidong successively took up the post. The Liangjiang Viceroy's Official Residence was located on the former site of the Prince Han's Residence of the Ming Dynasty. It was the Heavenly Dynasty Palace of the Taiping Heavenly Kingdom from 1853 to 1864. It was rebuilt after it.

清朝两江总督署东、西辕门，分书“三省钧衡”“两江保障”

East and West Outer Gate of the Liangjiang Viceroy's Official Residence Respectively with Chinese Characters: "San Sheng Jun Heng" (equilibrium of three provinces) and "Liang Jiang Bao Zhang" (Safeguarding Liangjiang)

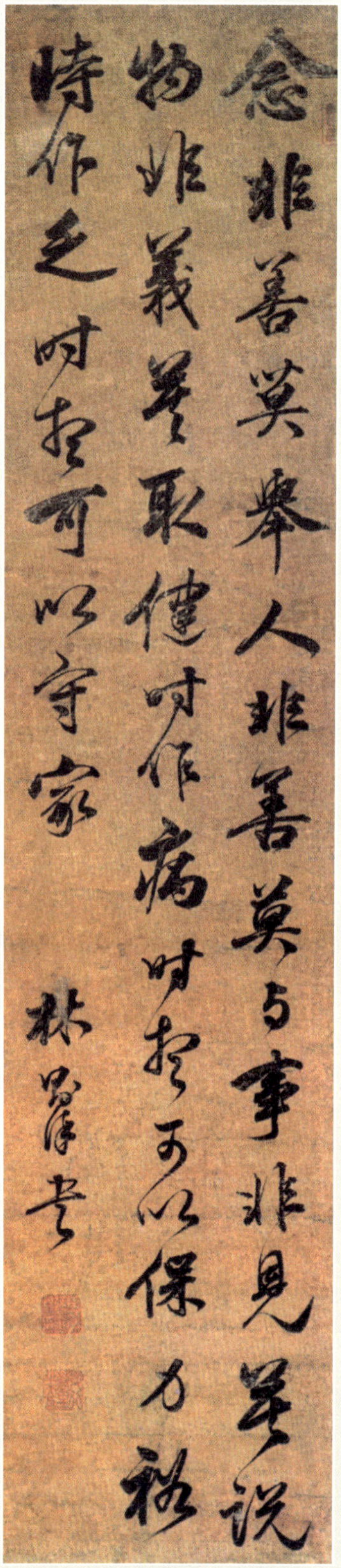

林则徐书写的行书

Calligraphy of Lin Zexu

林则徐，曾任两江总督，著名爱国政治家。厉行禁烟，主持“虎门销烟”，抵抗西方侵略

Lin Zexu, Liangjiang Viceroy, famous patriotic politician, presided over the burning of opium in Hoomun, Canton in 1839.

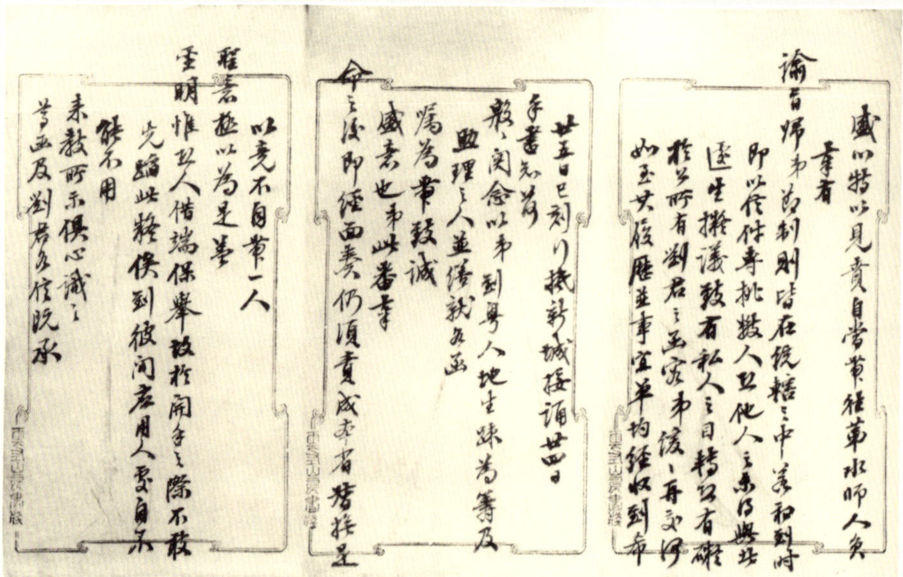

林则徐写给友人的信

Lin Zexu's Letter to His Friend

“印心石屋”石匾。1835 年，清道光皇帝题写“印心石屋”四字，赏赐给两江总督陶澍

Stone carved with Emperor Daoguang's inscriptions “Yinxinshi Wu” (heart shaped stone house) was rewarded to Tao Shu in 1835.

陶澍画像

陶澍，曾任两江总督。致力于治水，筹划海运， 革除盐政弊端

Tao Shu, Liangjiang Viceroy, devoted himself to water control, sea transportation, abuse of the salt administration.

于成龙，曾任两江总督。有“天下第一廉吏”之称

Yu Chenglong, Liangjiang Viceroy, Known as “the First Incorruptible Feudal Official Under Heaven ”

曾国藩，曾四任两江总督。著名政治家，中国近代军阀的创始人

Zeng Guofan, famous politician, one of the earliest warlords in modern China, who took the post of the Liangjiang Viceroy in four times.

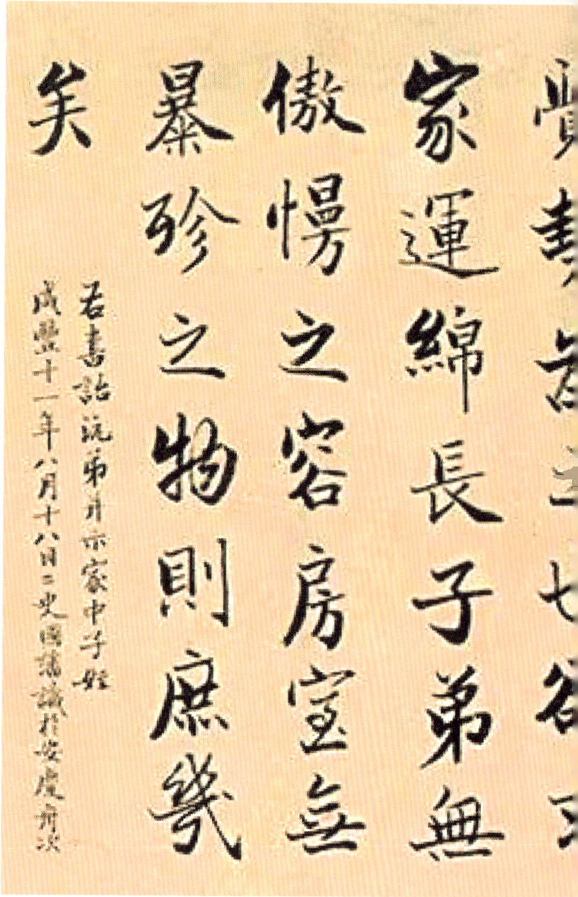

曾国藩手书家训

Zeng Guofan's calligraphy of family instructions

“勋高柱石”碑亭（今摄）。1870 年 10 月，清同治皇帝亲笔御赐“勋高柱石”四字赏给曾国藩做寿

“Xun Gao Zhu Shi” Tablet (Picture taken in the 2010s)

In October 1870, Emperor Tongzhi granted Zeng Guofan four Chinese characters: “Xun Gao Zhu Shi” (i.e. making great contributions for and the mainstay of the Qing Dynasty) for his suppression of the Taiping Troops.

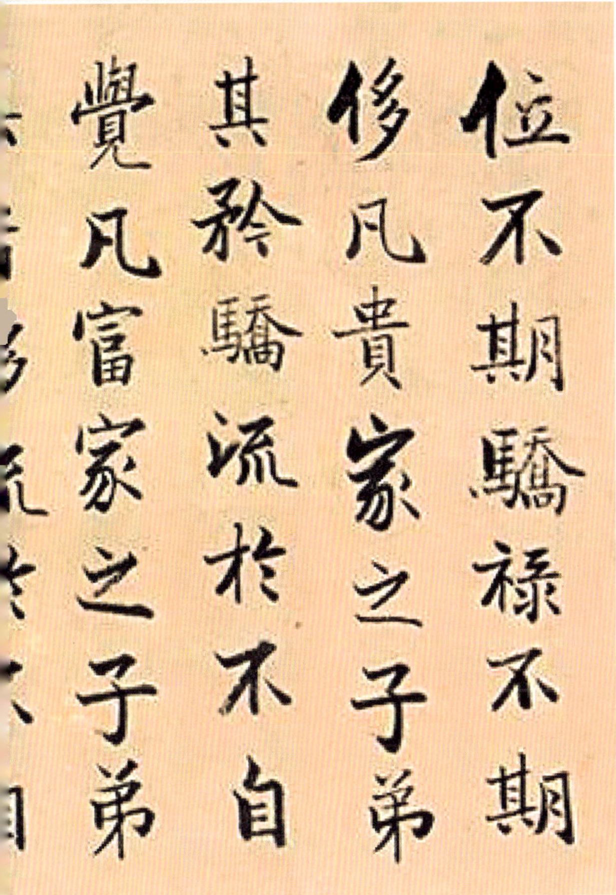

曾国荃，曾任两江总督，湘军将领。1864 年率军攻陷太平天国都城天京

Zeng Guoquan, Liangjiang Viceroy, who commanded Qing Troops to occupy Tianjing, capital of the Taiping Heavenly Kingdom in 1864.

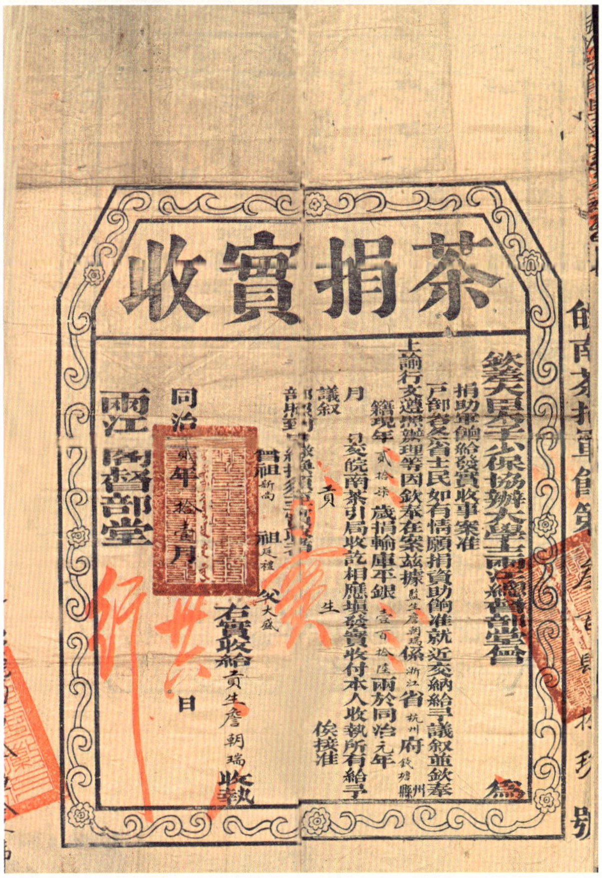

清同治年间，两江总督开具的收执

Receipt opened by the Liangjiang Viceroy in the Reign of Emperor Tongzhi

耆英，曾任两江总督。1842年8月，代表清政府与英国签订中英《江宁条约》（即《南京条约》），之后出任该职

Qiying (Keying), on behalf of the Qing Government signed the Jiangning Treaty (Nanjing Treaty) with the British in August 1842.

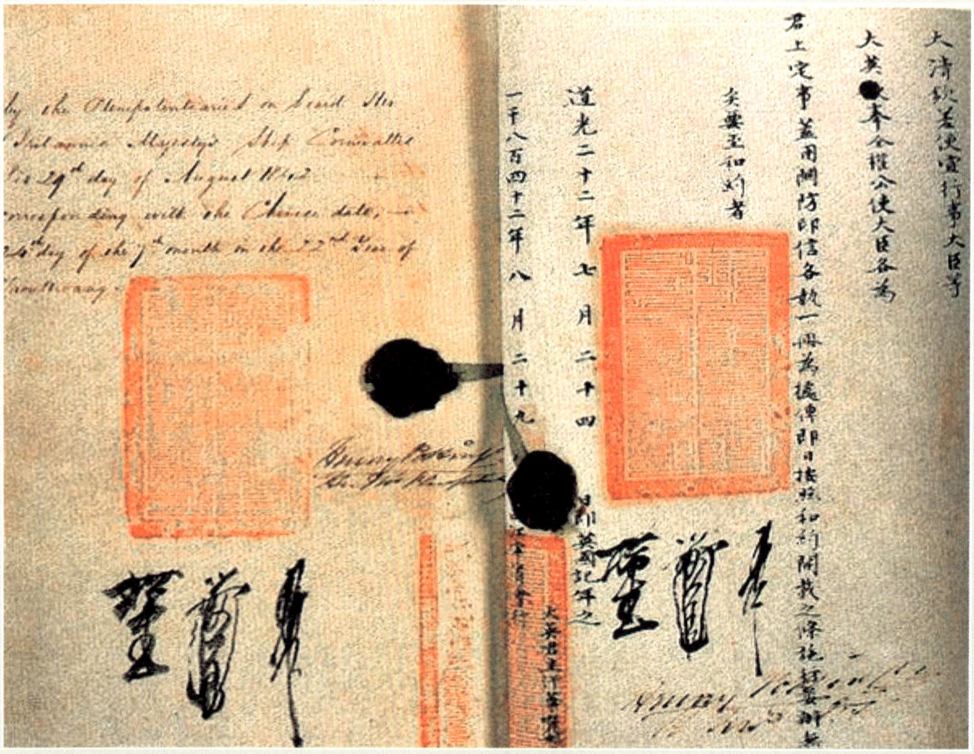

by the Plenipotentiaries on board Her Britannic Majesty's Ship Cornwallis this 29th day of August 1842 corresponding with the Chinese date, 24th day of the 7th month in the 22nd Year of Taoukwang

大清钦差便宜行事大臣等
大英□奉全权公使大臣各为
君上定事盖用关防印信各执一册为据俾即日按照和约开载之条施行
矣要至和约者
道光二十二年七月二十四
一千八百四十二年八月二十九

清朝钦差大臣耆英等与英国签订的《江宁条约》文本

Part of the Text of the Jiangning (Nanjing) Treaty

左宗棠，曾任两江总督。洋务派首领，率军收复新疆

Zuo Zongtang, Liangjiang Viceroy, one of leaders of the Westernization Movement, commanded troops to recover Xinjiang.

沈葆桢，曾任两江总督。任上兴修水利，整顿盐务，筹划海防。奉命率海陆军巡视台湾，迫使日军退出

Shen Baozhen, Liangjiang Viceroy, paid attention to irrigation, salt administration and coast defence. He commanded naval and military forces by order to inspect Taiwan and drove Japanese troops out of Taiwan in 1874.

刘坤一，曾任两江总督。甲午战争北洋水师兵败后，曾力主对日继续作战

Liu Kunyi, Liangjiang Viceroy, advocated to keep on fighting against Japan after the failure of Beiyang Navy in the War of 1894.

张之洞，曾任两江总督，洋务派代表人物之一。大力创办近代工业，编练江南自强军，支持维新运动

Zhang Zhidong, Liangjiang Viceroy, one of representatives of the Westernization Movement, who created modern industry, trained the Jiangnan Self-Strengthen Army, and donated to the Reform Movement.

张之洞在批阅公文

Zhang Zhidong Reviewing Documents

李鸿章，曾任两江总督。洋务派首领，国营招商局创办人

Li Hongzhang, Liangjiang Viceroy, one of leaders of the Westernization Movement and the originator of the China Merchants' Steamer Navigation Co. Ld.

李鸿章创建的金陵机器局

The Nanking Arsenal Set up by Li Hongzhang

魏光焘，曾任两江总督。在南京创办三江学堂，首开近代江苏高等教育之先河

Wei Guangtao, Liangjiang Viceroy, set up San Jiang College and initiated the higher education of Jiangsu province.

1903 年魏光焘在总督署煦园不系舟与宾客合影

Wei Guangtao took group photo with guests on "Bu Xi Zhou" (i.e. need-not-tether-boat) in the West Garden of the Liangjiang Viceroy's Official Residence in 1903.

端方，曾任两江总督。任上积极致力新政，开办南洋劝业会，筹建总督署西花厅

Duanfang, the Liangjiang Viceroy who paid attention to new political system, held Nanyang Exhibition, and prepared to build "Xi Hua Ting" (i.e. West Flower House).

清两江总督端方接见外国使节

Duanfang Meeting with Foreign Guests

张人骏，末任两江总督。任上在总督署建成西花厅（后为临时大总统办公室）。1911 年 12 月，在江浙联军光复南京之役中兵败

Zhang Renjun, the last Liangjiang Viceroy who completed the construction of "Xi Hua Ting" (which then became the Provisional Presidential Office) and fled after the occupation of Nanjing by the Jiangsu-Zhejiang Allied Army in December 1911.

清朝两江总督署东墙远眺（远处为"御书楼"，近处为宁省铁路及箭道车站）

Distant View of the East Wall of the Compound of the Liangjiang Viceroy's Official Residence

清朝官帽以官品高低缀有红宝石、珊瑚、蓝宝石等顶珠，并插有翎枝，分花翎、蓝翎两种，又称“顶戴花翎”

In the Qing Dynasty, official hat shows various ranks by button of precious stone on top, such as ruby, coral, sapphire et al. It was also called “Rank Button”.

清朝官员在朝服的前胸后背处分别缀有一块方形的图案，称作“补子”，用来表示官阶差异。文官绣禽，武将绣兽，文官、武将均设置九品十八级

In the Qing Dynasty, there were plaques of embroidery sewn on the breast and back of official court robes called “Buzi” (patch) which was an important mark to show the rank and official position. Usually, the civil officials’ robes were embroidered with birds, while the military officers’ robes were decorated with beasts.

清朝两江总督署西花园石舫，系乾隆十一年（1746年）两江总督尹继善为迎乾隆南巡所建。后乾隆题赐“不系舟”。近处为夕佳楼

The Stone Boat in the West Garden was originally built by the Liangjiang Viceroy Yin Jishan in order to welcome Emperor Qianlong in 1746. On Emperor Qianlong's second inspection tour to south China named it "Bu Xi Zhou" (need-not-tether-boat).

石舫（不系舟）（今摄）

Stone Boat (need-not-tether-boat) (Picture taken in the 2010s)

1870 年重修两江总督署时，在西花园中所建的中式园林建筑（今摄）

Chinese Garden Architecture Built in the West Garden in 1870 (Picture taken in the 2010s)

煦园

The Front Entrance of Xu Garden

桐音馆

Tong Yin Hall

花厅

Flower Hall

忘飞阁

Wang Fei (Forgetting-flying) Pavilion

夕佳楼

Xi Jia Tower

漪澜阁

Yi Lan Pavilion

敕治两江（油画）

Running Liangjiang in Obedience to Emperor's Order (Oil Painting)

三

共和肇始　孙文就任大总统

III. Initiation of the Republic and Provisional President Dr Sun Yat-sen's Oath on Taking Office

1911年10月，辛亥革命爆发。12月2日，江浙联军光复南京。12月29日，已独立的十七省代表在清江苏咨议局选举孙中山为中华民国临时大总统。1912年1月1日，孙中山在清两江总督署大堂宣誓就职，并在原总督署设立总统府。孙中山创建了共和制的国家政权——中华民国临时政府，进行了一系列政治、军事、经济、法制和社会变革，并组织北伐。清帝退位后，孙中山辞去了临时大总统一职，于4月3日解职离开总统府。孙中山在总统府工作、生活了94天。

Following the Wuchang Uprising in October 1911, the Jiang (su)-Zhe (jiang) Allied Army occupied Nanjing on 2 December 1911. Dr. Sun Yat-sen was elected Provisional President of the Republic of China by the seventeen independent provincial military governors or their representatives in the Jiangsu Provincial Assembly on 29 December 1911. On 1 January 1912, Dr. Sun Yat-sen was sworn in as Provisional President of the Republic of China in the former Liangjiang Viceroy's Official Residence. The first republican government in Chinese history—the Nanjing Provisional Government was founded. It promulgated a series of important influential policies in politic, military, economics, laws and society. Dr. Sun Yat-sen organized the Northern Expedition. Provisional President Sun Yat-sen resigned the presidency after the abdication of the last Emperor of the Qing Dynasty and left the Presidential Office on 3 April 1912. Dr. Sun Yat-sen worked and lived a total of 94 days in the Presidential Office.

1911年12月2日，江浙联军光复南京，图为联军攻入仪凤门

The Jiang (su) -Zhe (jiang) Allied Army attacked Yifeng Gate and entered Nanjing on 2 December 1911.

南京光复之役中的联军炮兵占领天保城

The Occupation of Tianbaocheng of Nanjing by the Artillery of the Jiang (su) -Zhe (jiang) Allied Army

江浙联军总司令徐绍桢

Xu Shaozhen, Commander-in-Chief of the Jiang (su) -Zhe (jiang) Allied Army

光复后的清两江总督署辕门

Outer Gate of the Liangjiang Viceroy's Official Residence after the Recovery of Nanjing

镇军都督林述庆率军最先攻入南京

Lin Shuqing commanded the Zhenjiang Revolutionary Army first occupied Nanjing.

林述庆在原两江总督署设立林都督行辕

Field Headquarters of Lin Shuqing, Commander of the Zhenjiang Revolutionary Army

1911年12月，江浙联军官兵在清两江总督署西花园石舫留影

Officers and men of the Jiang (su) –Zhe (jiang) Allied Army Posed on the Stone Boat in the Liangjiang Viceroy's Official Residence in December 1911.

光复后的清两江总督署大堂

The Hall of the First Row of Houses of the Liangjiang Viceroy's Official Residence after the Recovery of Nanjing

1911年12月21日，孙中山回国途中在船上与欢迎者合影

Dr. Sun Yat-sen posted for a group photo with the welcoming party on board the steamer while he arrived in Hongkong on 21 December 1911.

1911年12月26日，孙中山与黄兴等人在上海哈同花园召开同盟会干部会议，密商国体问题

Dr. Sun Yat-sen and Huang Xing et al. held a meeting of cadres of the China Federal Association to discuss the state system at Hardoon Garden, Shanghai, on 26 December 1911.

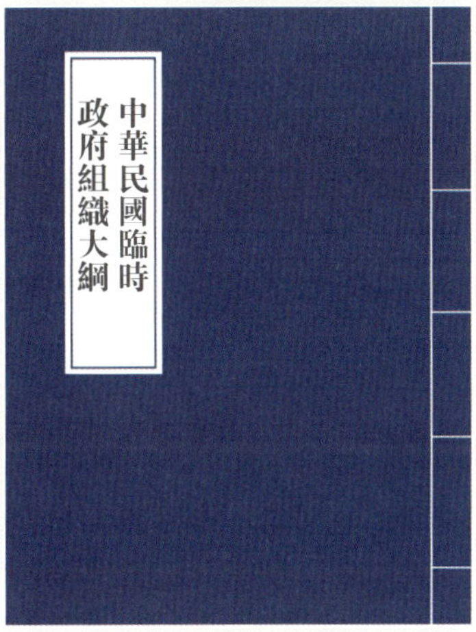

《中华民国临时政府组织大纲》文本

Organic Rules of the Provisional Government of the Republican China

1911 年 12 月 30 日，孙中山在上海同生照相馆拍摄的标准像

Dr. Sun Yat-sen's Official Portrait Posed by Shanghai Tongsheng Photo Studio on 30 December 1911

副总统黎元洪

Vice President Li Yuanhong

1911 年 12 月 29 日，已独立的十七省代表在原清江苏咨议局，经两轮投票，选举孙中山为中华民国临时大总统，黎元洪为副总统。这是选举会的合影

Dr. Sun Yat-sen was elected Provisional President of the Republican China by the seventeen independent provincial generals or their representatives in the Jiangsu Provincial Assembly on 29 December 1911. Provisional President Sun Yat-sen had a photograph taken with the representatives who attended the election meeting.

临时大总统府办公室全景（总督署西花厅）

Full View of the Provisional President's Official Residence (West Flower Garden of the Liangjiang Viceroy's Official Residence)

临时大总统办公室（侧影）

Provisional President's Office (Sideview)

临时大总统办公室（今摄）

Provisional President's Office (Picture taken in the 2010s)

1912 年 1 月 1 日晚 11 时，孙中山在各省代表、中外友人、新闻界的见证下，宣誓就任中华民国临时大总统。这是就职时的孙中山

Dr. Sun Yat-sen was sworn in as the Provisional President of the Republican China at 11 p.m. on 1 January 1912.

“中华民国临时大总统印”印文

Seal of the President of the Provisional Government of the Republican China

孙中山宣誓就职的清两江总督署（总统府）大堂（今摄）

The Hall of the First Row of Houses of the Liangjiang Viceroy's Official Residence where Dr. Sun Yat-sen was sworn in as the Provisional President of the Republican China (Picture taken in the 2010s).

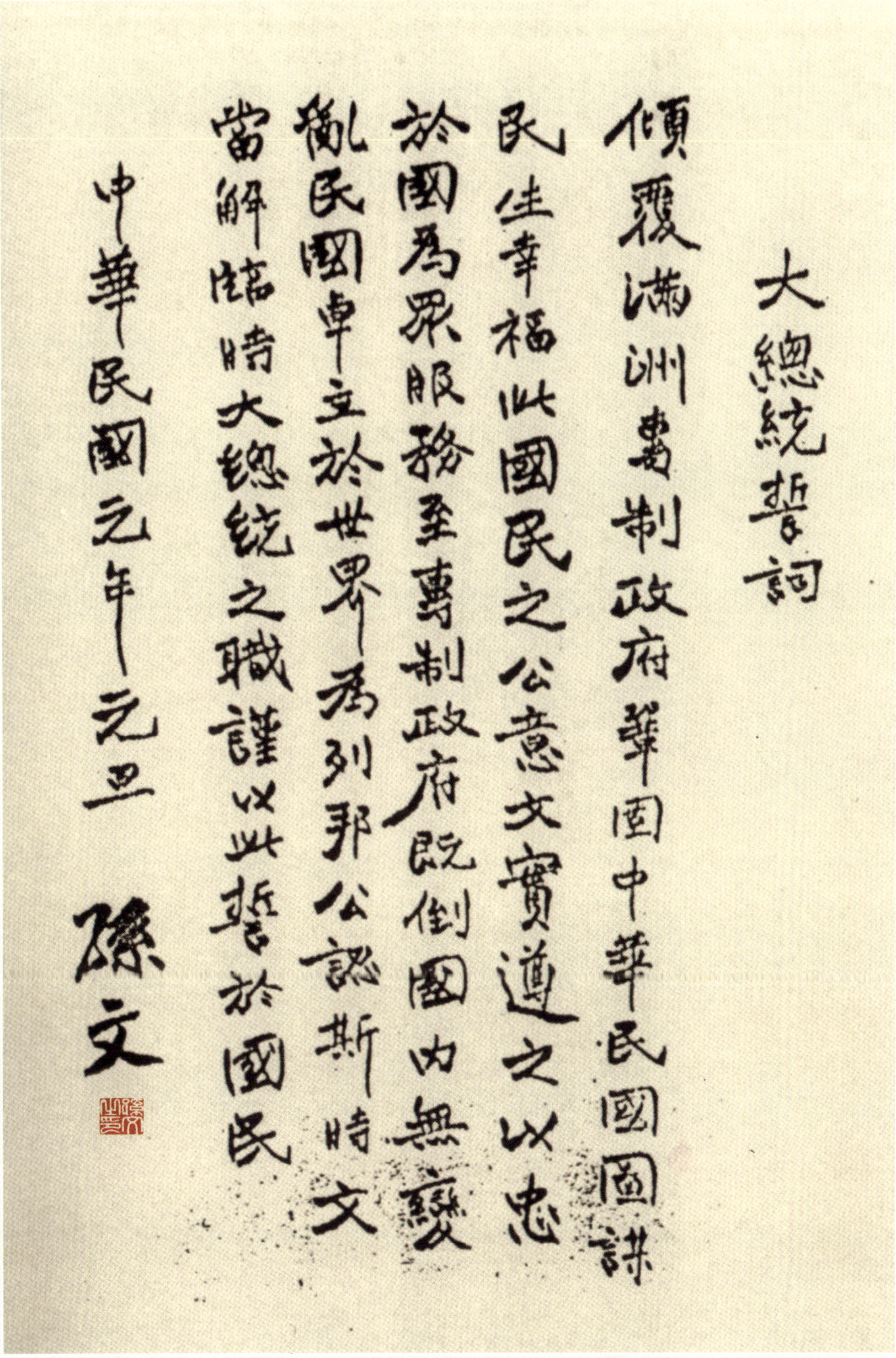
大總統誓詞

傾覆滿洲專制政府鞏固中華民國圖謀
民生幸福此國民之公意文實遵之以忠
於國為眾服務至專制政府既倒國內無變
亂民國卓立於世界為列邦公認斯時文
當解臨時大總統之職謹以此誓於國民

中華民國元年元旦 孫文

大总统誓词

The Oath of the Provisional President

孙中山与儿子孙科（参加中华民国开国典礼时摄）

Dr. Sun Yat-sen with His Son Sun Fo (Picture taken in the founding ceremony of the Republican China)

就职典礼结束后，孙中山与同仁合影

Dr. Sun Yat-sen posed for a group photo with his colleagues after his inauguration.

纪念民国成立明信片

Postcard Issued by the Nanjing Provisional Government

民国成立宣传画

Picture Poster on the Founding of the Republic of China

民国元年月份牌

Calendar of the First Year of the Republic of China

南京总统府大门，高悬五色旗和十八星旗

Five-Colour Flag (Rainbow Flag) and Red Eighteen-Star Flag Hanging over the Gate of the Nanjing Provisional Government

1912 年 2 月 5 日，孙中山在内阁会议后留影

President Sun Yat-sen after the Cabinet Meeting on 5 February 1912

南京临时政府总长会议室（今摄）

Minister's Meeting Room of the Nanjing Provisional Government (Picture taken in the 2010s)

1912 年 1 月 21 日，孙中山在总统府总长会议室（西花厅）主持召开第一次内阁会议。因部分总长未到任，多由次长掌权，故有“次长内阁”之称

President Sun Yat-sen presided over the first Cabinet meeting at the minister's meeting room on 21 January 1912. Since some of the ministers had not yet arrived in Nanjing to take office, the vice-ministers were temporarily in charge of ministries, so it was called the "vice-minister cabinet".

孙中山与部分内阁成员合影

President Sun Yat-sen Posing for a Group Photo with the Cabinet Members

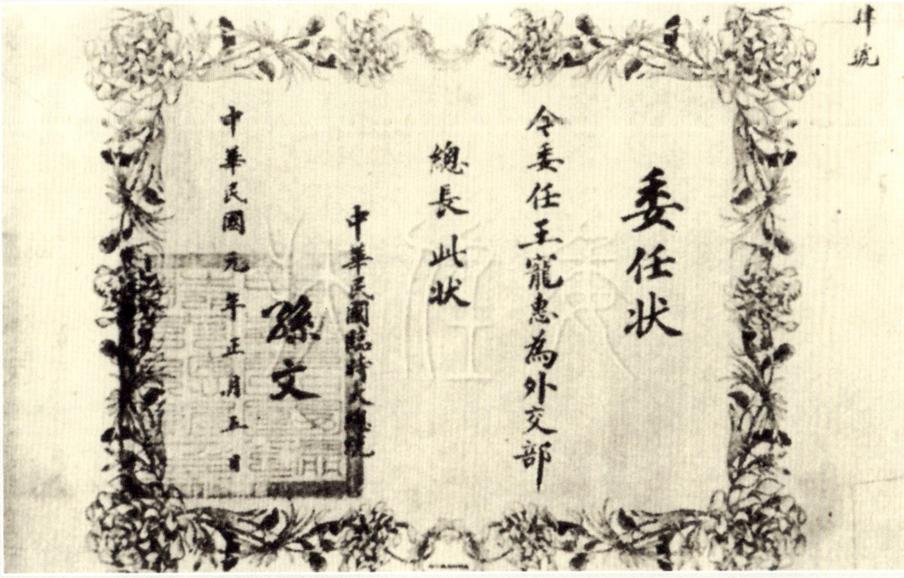

肆號

委任狀

令委任王寵惠為外交部
總長此狀

中華民國臨時大總統
孫文
中華民國元年正月五日

孙中山颁发给王宠惠的委任状

Certificate of Appointment to Wang Chonghui Issued by President Sun Yat-sen

陆军部总长兼参谋部总长黄兴

Huang Xing, Minister of War

陆军部次长蒋作宾

Jiang Zuobin, Vice-Minister of War

海军部总长黄钟瑛

Huang Zhongying, Minister of Navy

海军部次长汤芗铭

Tang Xiangming, Vice-Minister of Navy

内务部总长程德全

Cheng Dequan, Minister of Interior Affairs

内务部次长居正

Ju Zheng, Vice-Minister of Interior Affairs

外交部总长王宠惠

Wang Chonghui, Minister of Foreign Affairs

外交部次长魏宸组

Wei Chenzu, Vice-Minister of Foreign Affairs

财政部总长陈锦涛

Chen Jintao, Minister of Finance

财政部次长王鸿猷

Wang Hongyou, Vice-Minister of Finance

教育部总长蔡元培

Cai Yuanpei, Minister of Education

教育部次长景耀月

Jing Yaoyue, Vice-Minister of Education

司法部总长伍廷芳

Wu Tingfang, Minister of Justice

司法部次长吕志伊

Lü Zhiyi, Vice-Minister of Justice

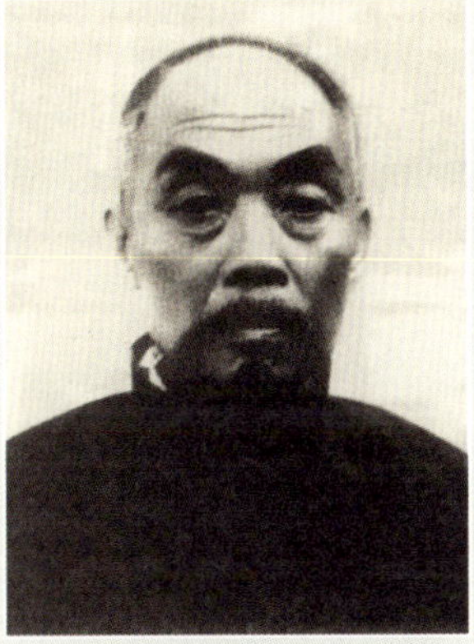

实业部总长张謇

Zhang Jian, Minister of Industry

实业部次长马君武

Ma Junwu, Vice-Minister of Industry

交通部总长汤寿潜

Tang Shouqian, Minister of Communications

交通部次长于右任

Yu Youren, Vice-Minister of Communications

参谋部次长钮永建

Niu Yongjian, Deputy Chief of General Staff

南京卫戍总督徐绍桢

Xu Shaozhen, Governor of Nanjing Garrison

总统府美籍军事顾问荷马李将军

General Homer Lea, American Adviser to the Nanjing Provisional Government

总统府日籍政治顾问宫崎寅藏

Toten Miyazaki, Japanese Political Adviser to the Nanjing Provisional Government

孙中山、胡汉民等与秘书处官员合影

President Sun Yat-sen Posing for a Group Photo with Hu Hanmin and Officials of the Secretariat

总统府秘书长胡汉民

Hu Hanmin, Secretary-General of the Nanjing Provisional Government

总统府秘书处

Secretariat of the Nanjing Provisional Government

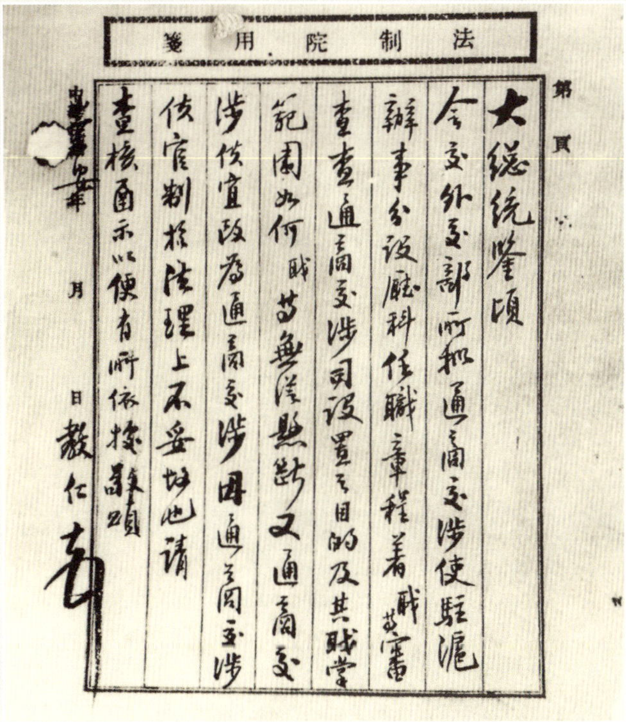

法制院用箋

第 頁

大總統鑒頃
令交外交部所擬通商交涉使駐滬
辦事分設廳科任職章程着戰審
查通商交涉司設置之目的及其職掌
範圍如何戰若無從懸斷又通商交
涉使宜改為通商交涉司因通商交涉
使官制於法理上不妥故也請
查核函示以便有所依據擬辦

中華民國元年 月 日 教仁

法制局长宋教仁致孙中山关于涉外事务的信

Song Jiaoren's Message to Sun Yat-sen Concerning Foreign Affairs

法制局长宋教仁

Song Jiaoren, Director of the Bureau of Legislation

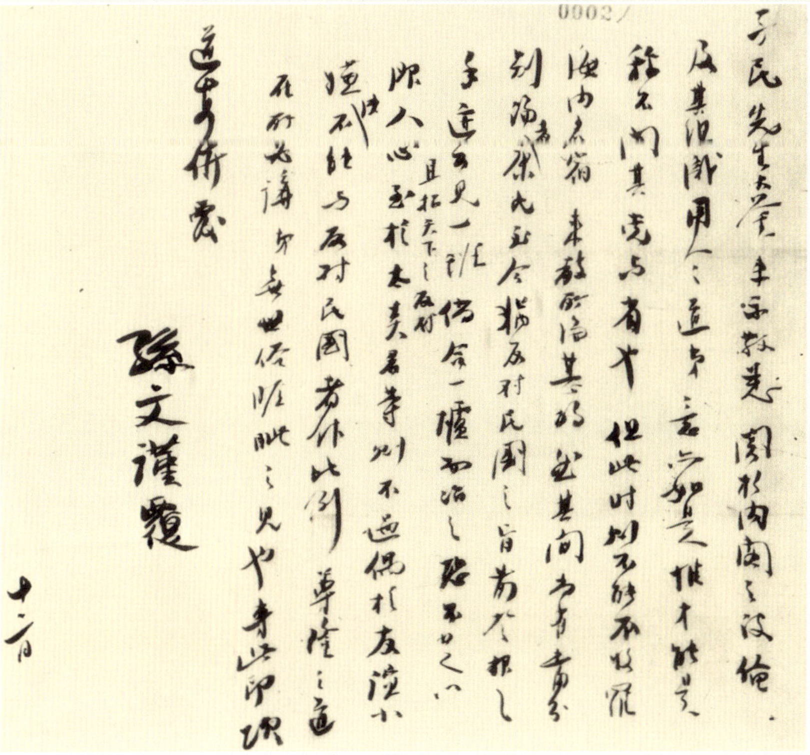

孙中山复教育总长蔡元培的函

President Sun Yat-sen's Message in Replying to Cai Yuanpei, Minister of Education

1912年1月9日，孙中山、黄兴与陆军部官佐合影

President Sun Yat-sen posed for a group photo with Huang Xing and officers of the Ministry of War on 9 January 1912.

1912年1月9日，孙中山、黄兴与参谋部官佐合影

President Sun Yat-sen posed for a group photo with Huang Xing and officers of the General Staff on 9 January 1912.

临时政府财政部

Ministry of Finance of the Nanjing Provisional Government

临时政府教育部

Ministry of Education of the Nanjing Provisional Government

1912 年 1 月 28 日，中华民国临时参议院成立合影

President Sun Yat-sen attended the formal opening of the Senate of the Nanjing Provisional Government on 28 January 1912. He posed for a group photo with the senators.

1912 年的中华民国临时参议院

The Provisional Senate of the Republic of China in 1912

临时参议院议长林森

Lin Sen, President of the Senate of the Nanjing Provisional Government

副议长、议和参赞王正廷

Wang Zhengting, Counsellor of the South-North Peace Negotiations

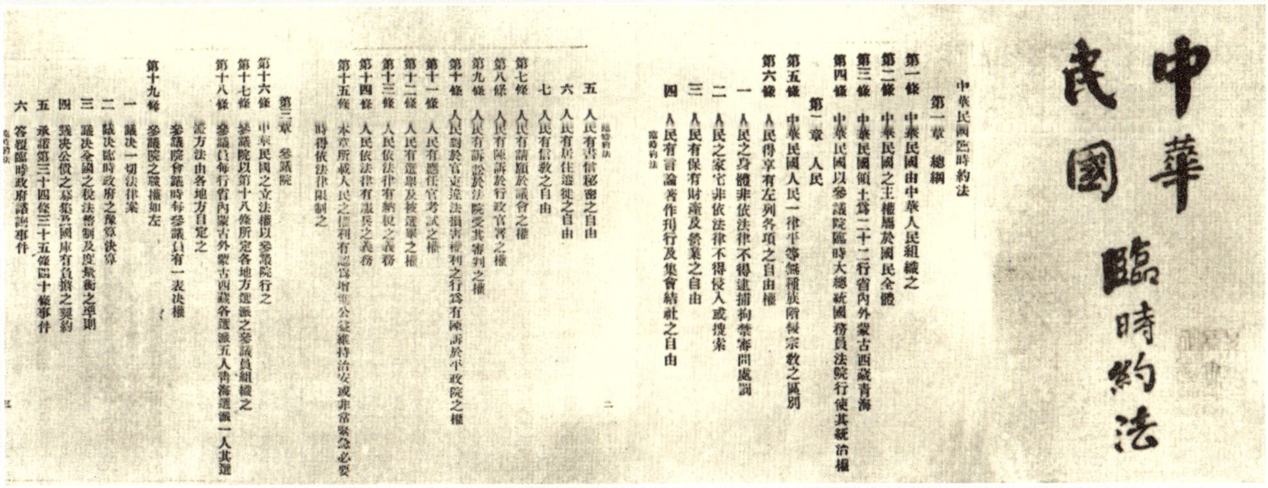

中華民國
臨時約法

中華民國臨時約法

第一章 總綱

第一條 中華民國由中華人民組織之

第二條 中華民國之主權屬於國民全體

第三條 中華民國領土爲二十二行省內外蒙古西藏青海

第四條 中華民國以參議院臨時大總統國務員法院行使其統治權

第二章 人民

第五條 中華民國人民一律平等無種族階級宗教之區別

第六條 人民得享有左列各項之自由權

一 人民之身體非依法律不得逮捕拘禁審問處罰

二 人民之家宅非依法律不得侵入或搜索

三 人民有保有財產及營業之自由

四 人民有言論著作刊行及集會結社之自由

五 人民有書信秘密之自由

六 人民有居住遷徙之自由

七 人民有信教之自由

第七條 人民有請願於議會之權

第八條 人民有陳訴於行政官署之權

第九條 人民有訴訟於法院受其審判之權

第十條 人民對於官吏違法損害權利之行爲有陳訴於平政院之權

第十一條 人民有應任官考試之權

第十二條 人民有選舉及被選舉之權

第十三條 人民依法律有納稅之義務

第十四條 人民依法律有服兵之義務

第十五條 本章所載人民之權利有認爲增進公益維持治安或非常緊急必要時得依法律限制之

第三章 參議院

第十六條 中華民國之立法權以參議院行之

第十七條 參議院以第十八條所定各地方選派之參議員組織之

第十八條 參議員每行省內蒙古外蒙古西藏各選派五人青海選派一人其選派方法由各地方自定之

參議院會議時每參議員有一表決權

第十九條 參議院之職權如左

一 議決一切法律案

二 議決臨時政府之預算決算

三 議決全國之稅法幣制及度量衡之準則

四 議決公債之募集及國庫有負擔之契約

五 承諾第三十四條三十五條四十條事件

六 答覆臨時政府諮詢事件

《中华民国临时约法》文本

The Provisional Constitution of the Republic of China

临时参议院议决，以五色旗为民国国旗。五色，寓意汉满蒙回藏“五族共和”

The Resolution of the Meeting of the Provisional Senate: The Five-Colour Flag Symbolizing the Republicanism of Han, Man, Meng, Hui, Zang Nationalities as the National Flag of the Republican China

民国陆军旗铁血十八星旗

The Red Eighteen-Star Flag as the Flag of the Army of the Republican China

民国海军旗青天白日旗

The Blue Sky and White Sun Flag as the Flag of Navy of the Republican China

清朝黄龙旗成为历史

Yellow Dragon Flag of the Qing Government

孙中山在总统府

President Sun Yat-sen at the President's Office

孙中山与总统府职员合影

President Sun Yat-sen Posing for a Group Photo with Staff of the Provisional Government

女子北伐队首领林宗雪

Lin Zongxue, Commander-in-Chief of the Chinese Republican Amazon Corps

北伐军关外大都督蓝天蔚

Lan Tianwei, Commander-in-Chief of the Northern Expeditionary Army

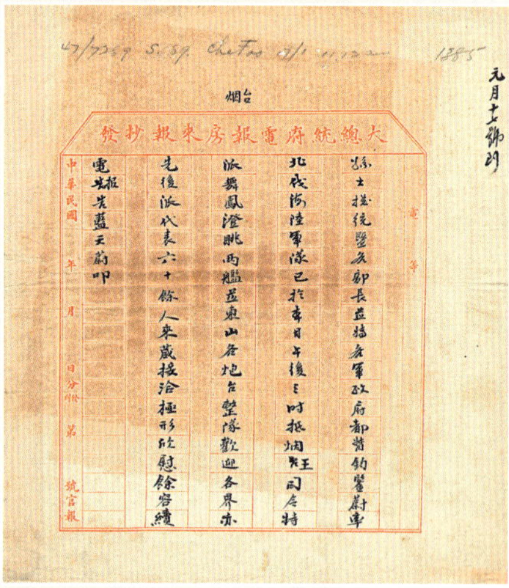

47/7259 S.59. Chefoo 21/1 11.12

1885

元月十七號到

台烟

大總統府電報房來報抄發

孫大總統暨各部長並轉各軍政府都督鈞鑒蔚率
北伐海陸軍隊已於本日午後三時抵烟台同人特
派舞鳳澄雎兩艦並東山各炮台整隊歡迎各界亦
先後派代表六十餘人來藏接洽極形欣慰餘容續
電告藍天蔚叩

中華民國 年 月 日 分 時 第 號 官報

蓝天蔚就北伐途中战况致孙中山等电

Lan Tianwei's Telegram to President Sun Yat-sen et al. Reporting on the Situation on the Battlefield

孙中山担任大总统后，立即筹划北伐大计，组建陆海空三军，直指清政府。图为整装待发的北伐军官兵

President Sun Yat-sen immediately organized army, navy and air forces to prepare for the northern expedition to attack the Qing Government. The photograph shows that the officers and men were fully equipped for the Northern Expedition.

北伐海军舰队“海容”号

“Hai Rong” Chinese Republican Man-of-War for the Northern Expeditionary Army

北伐军敢死队

Death Squads of the Northern Expeditionary Army

总统府飞机队

Air Forces of the Nanjing Provisional Government

剪辫后的孙中山，身着中山装

Dr. Sun Yat-sen after Cutting off Pigtail and Wearing a “Zhongshan” Suit

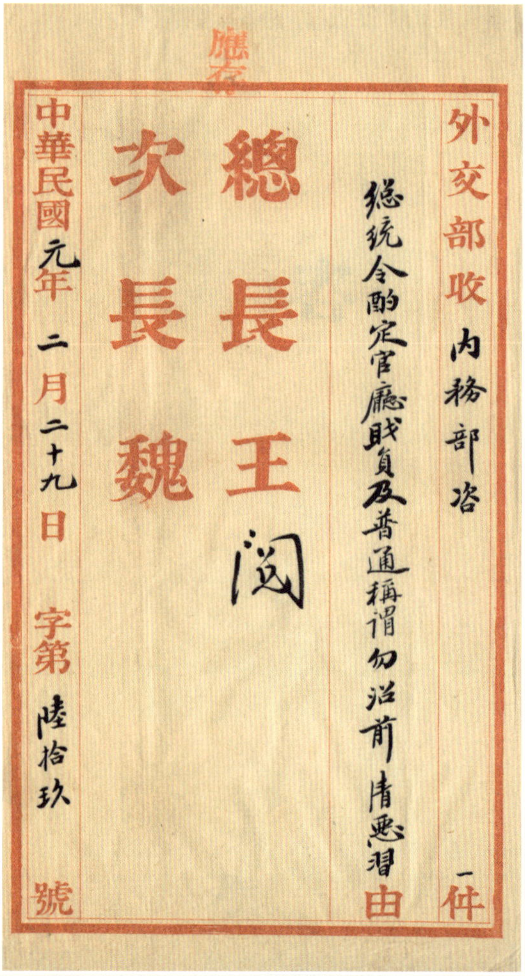

應存

外交部收 内務部咨 一件

總統令酌定官廳職員及普通稱謂勿沿前清惡習由

總長王 閱

次長魏

中華民國元年 二月二十九日

字第 陸拾玖 號

外交部收内务部“废除清朝恶习”的咨文

Official Message of the Ministry of Interior Affairs to the Ministry of Foreign Affairs Concerning the Abolition of Feudal and Irrational Practices of the Qing Dynasty

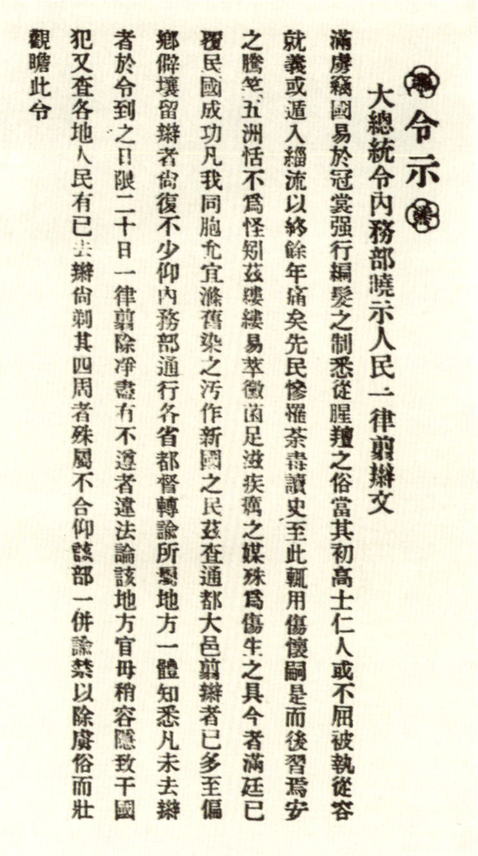

令示

大總統令內務部曉示人民一律剪辮文

滿虜竊國易於冠裳强行編髮之制悉從腥羶之俗當其初高士仁人或不屈被執從容
就義或遁入緇流以終餘年痛矣先民慘罹荼毒讀史至此輒用傷懷嗣是而後習爲安
之騰笑五洲恬不爲怪矧茲縷縷易萃黴菌足滋疾癘之媒殊爲傷生之具今者滿廷已
覆民國成功凡我同胞允宜滌舊染之汚作新國之民茲查通都大邑剪辮者已多至偏
鄉僻壤留辮者尙復不少仰內務部通行各省都督轉諭所屬地方一體知悉凡未去辮
者於令到之日限二十日一律剪除淨盡有不遵者違法論該地方官毋稍容隱致干國
犯又查各地人民有已去辮尙剃其四周者殊屬不合仰該部一併諭禁以除虜俗而壯
觀瞻此令

剪辫通令

Circular Order Concerning Cutting Pigtail

军人上街执行“剪辫通令”

Army-men Cutting Pigtail for Civilians in the Street

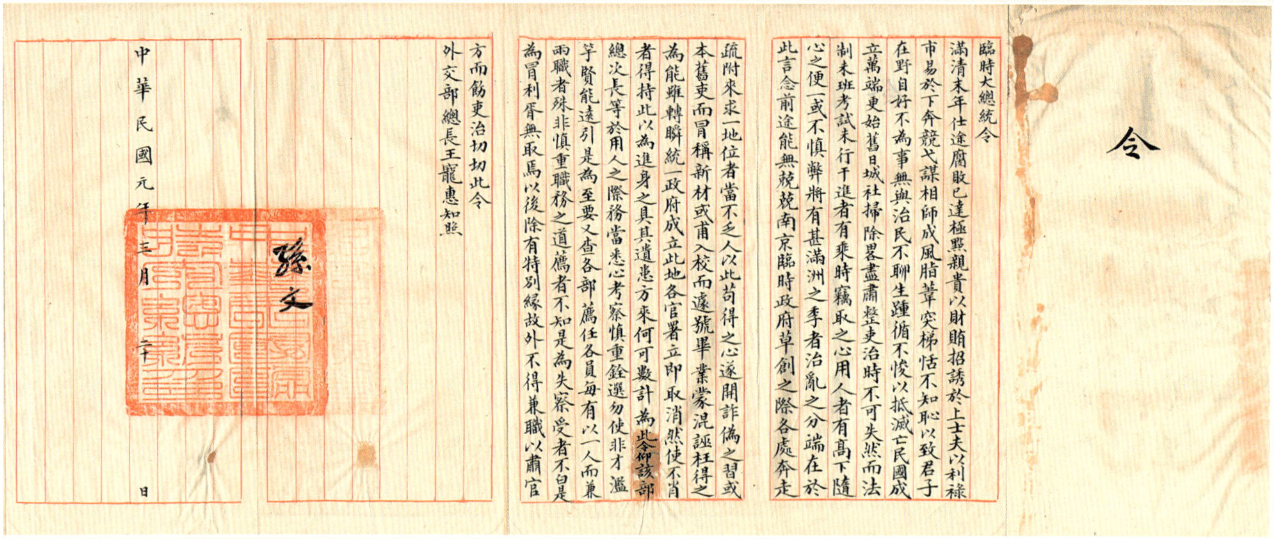
令

臨時大總統令
滿清末年仕途腐敗已達極點親貴以財賄招誘於上士夫以利祿
市易於下奔競弋謀相師成風脂韋突梯恬不知恥以致君子
在野自好不為事無與治民不聊生踵循不悛以抵滅亡民國成
立萬端更始舊日城社掃除畧盡肅整吏治時不可失然而法
制未班考試未行干進者有乘時竊取之心用人者有高下隨
心之便一或不慎弊將有甚滿洲之季者治亂之分端在於
此言念前途能無兢兢南京臨時政府草創之際各處奔走
疏附來求一地位者當不乏人以此苟得之心遂開詐偽之習或
本舊吏而冒稱新材或甫入校而遽號畢業蒙混誣枉得之
為能雖轉瞬統一政府成立此地各官署立即取消然使不肖
者得持此以為進身之具其遺患方來何可數計為此令仰該部
總次長等於用人之際務當悉心考察慎重銓選勿使非才濫
竽賢能遠引是為至要又查各部薦任各員每有以一人而兼
兩職者殊非慎重職務之道薦者不知是為失察受者不自是
為冒利胥無取焉以後除有特别緣故外不得兼職以肅官
方而飭吏治切切此令
外交部總長王寵惠知照

孫文

中華民國元年三月二十日

孙中山签发的“整顿吏治令”

President Sun Yat-sen's Order Emphasizing the Importance of Being Prudent in Selection of Officials

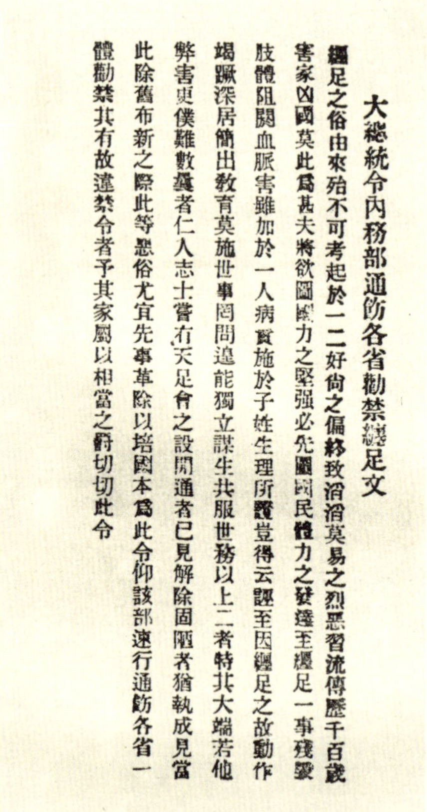
大總統令內務部通飭各省勸禁纏足文
纏足之俗由來殆不可考起於一二好尚之偏終致滔滔莫易之烈惡習流傳歷千百歲
害家凶國莫此爲甚夫將欲圖國力之堅強必先圖國民體力之發達至纏足一事殘毀
肢體阻閼血脈害雖加於一人病實施於子姓生理所證豈得云誣至因纏足之故動作
竭蹶深居簡出教育莫施世事罔問遑能獨立謀生共服世務以上二者特其大端若他
弊害更僕難數曩者仁人志士嘗有天足會之設開通者已見解除固陋者猶執成見當
此除舊布新之際此等惡俗尤宜先事革除以培國本爲此令仰該部速行通飭各省一
體勸禁其有故違禁令者予其家屬以相當之罰切切此令

禁止缠足通令

Circular Order Concerning the Prohibition of Foot-Binding

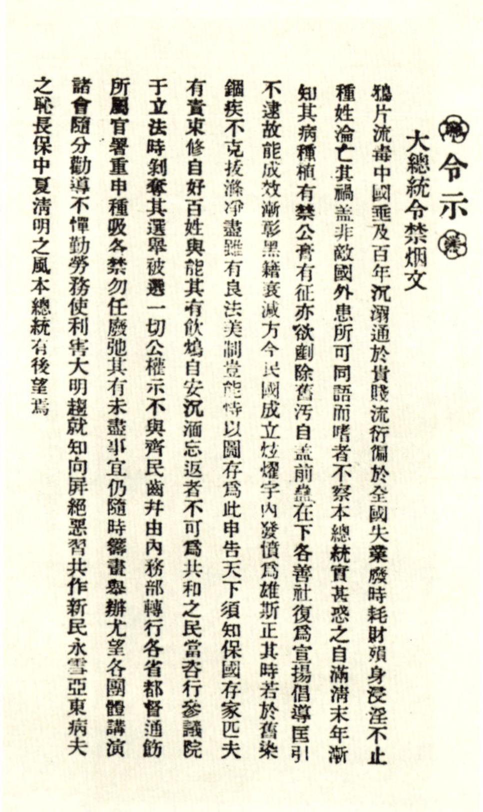
令示
大總統令禁烟文
鴉片流毒中國垂及百年沉溺通於貴賤流衍偏於全國失業廢時耗財殞身浸淫不止
種姓淪亡其禍蓋非敵國外患所可同語而嗜者不察本總統實甚悉之自滿清末年漸
知其病種植有禁公膏有征亦欲剷除舊汚自蓋前愆在下各善社復爲宣揚倡導匡引
不逮故能成效漸彰黑籍衰減方今民國成立炫燿宇內發憤爲雄斯正其時若於舊染
錮疾不克拔滌淨盡雖有良法美制豈能恃以圖存爲此申告天下須知保國存家匹夫
有責束修自好百姓與能其有飲鴆自安沉湎忘返者不可爲共和之民當咨行參議院
于立法時剝奪其選舉被選一切公權示不與齊民齒幷由內務部轉行各省都督通飭
所屬官署重申種吸各禁勿任廢弛其有未盡事宜仍隨時籌畫舉辦尤望各團體講演
諸會隨分勸導不憚勤勞務使利害大明趨就知向屏絕惡習共作新民永雪亞東病夫
之恥長保中夏清明之風本總統有後望焉

禁烟通令

Circular Order Concerning the Suppression of Opium

孙中山的大总统办公室

President Sun Yat-sen's Office

孙中山与卫士

President Sun Yat-sen with Bodyguards

民国时期的孙中山起居室

President Sun Yat-sen's Former Residence (Picture taken in the 1930s)

孙中山起居室（今摄）

President Sun Yat-sen's Former Residence (Picture taken in the 2010s)

孙中山与夫人偕儿女及宋蔼龄合影

Dr. Sun Yat-sen Posing for a Group Photo with His Wife, Daughter, and Soong Ailing

孙中山夫人卢慕贞

Lu Muzhen, Dr. Sun Yat-sen's Wife

孙中山的儿子孙科，女儿孙婉、孙娫

Dr. Sun Yat-sen's Children: Son Sun Fo, Daughters Sun Wan and Sun Yan

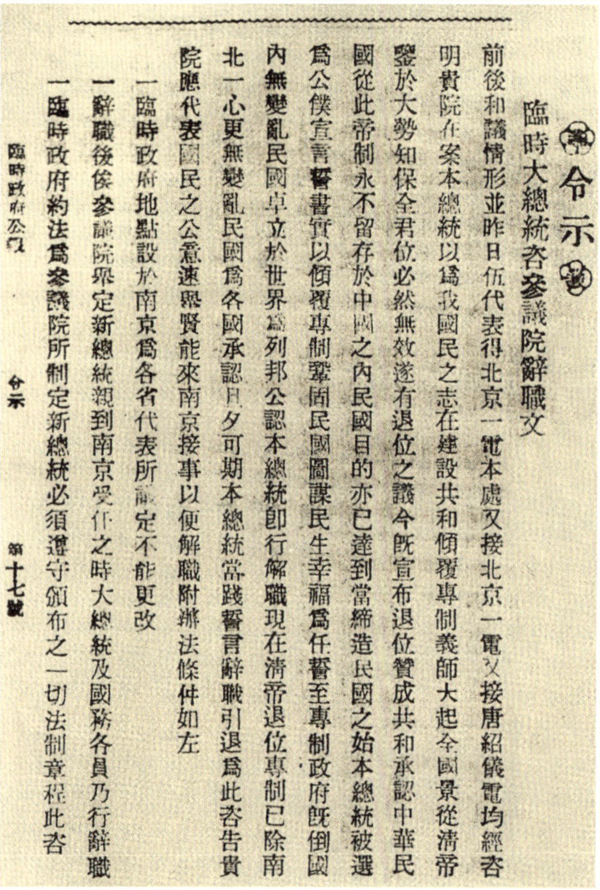

令示

臨時大總統咨參議院辭職文

前後和議情形並昨日伍代表得北京一電本處又接北京一電又接唐紹儀電均經咨明貴院在案本總統以爲我國民之志在建設共和傾覆專制義師大起全國景從清帝鑒於大勢知保全君位必然無效遂有退位之議今既宣布退位贊成共和承認中華民國從此帝制永不留存於中國之內民國目的亦已達到當締造民國之始本總統被選爲公僕宣言誓書實以傾覆專制鞏固民國圖謀民生幸福爲任誓至專制政府既倒國內無變亂民國卓立於世界爲列邦公認本總統即行解職現在清帝退位專制已除南北一心更無變亂民國爲各國承認旦夕可期本總統當踐誓言辭職引退爲此咨告貴院應代表國民之公意速舉賢能來南京接事以便解職附辦法條件如左

一臨時政府地點設於南京爲各省代表所議定不能更改

一辭職後俟參議院舉定新總統親到南京受任之時大總統及國務各員乃行辭職

一臨時政府約法爲參議院所制定新總統必須遵守頒布之一切法制章程此咨

臨時政府公報　令示　第十七號

清帝退位后，孙中山为履行诺言，辞去临时大总统一职，这是他向参议院提出的辞职咨文

President Sun Yat-sen's Resignation Message to the Provisional Senate

孙中山辞职后，在胡氏花园留影

Resigned President Sun Yat-sen in the Hus' Garden

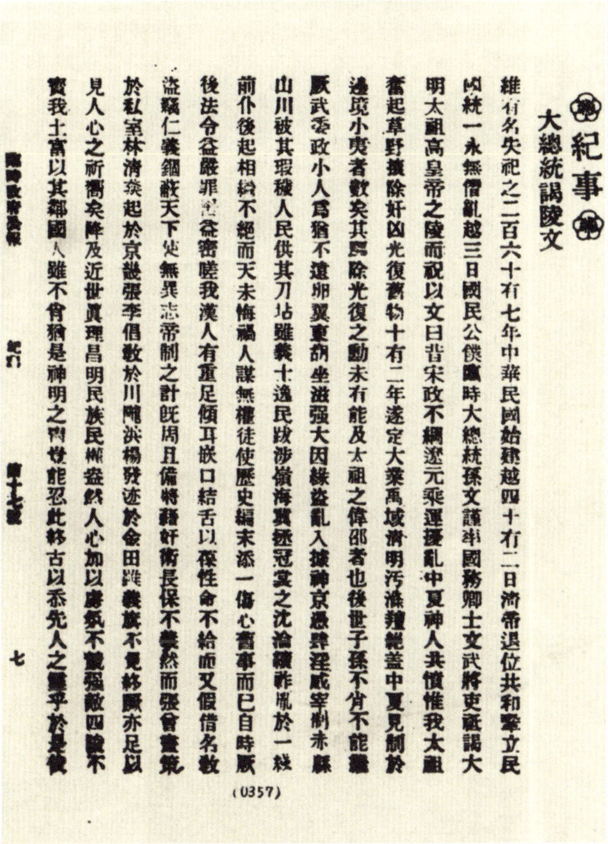

紀事

大總統謁陵文

維有名失祀之二百六十有七年中華民國始建越四十有二日清帝退位共和肇立民國統一永無僭亂越三日國民公僕臨時大總統孫文謹率國務卿士文武將吏祗謁大明太祖高皇帝之陵而祝以文曰昔宋政不綱遼元乘運擾亂中夏神人共憤惟我太祖奮起草野攘除奸凶光復舊物十有二年遂定大業禹域清明污濊蕩滌蓋中夏見制於邊境小夷者數矣其驅除光復之勳未有能及太祖之偉邵者也後世子孫不肖不能纘厥武委政小人爲猶不遠朔翼東胡坐滋强大因緣盜亂入據神京憑肆淫威宰制赤縣山川被其瑕穢人民供其刀砧雖義士逸民跋涉嶺海冀拯冠裳之沈淪續祚胤於一綫前仆後起相繼不絕而天未悔禍人謀無權徒使歷史編末添一傷心耆事而已自時厥後法令益嚴罪罟益密嗟我漢人有重足傾耳緘口結舌以葆性命不給而又假借名教盜竊仁義錮蔽天下使無異志帝制之計既周且備將藉奸術長保不替然而發憤變策於私室林清奕起於京畿張李倡教於川陝洪楊發迹於金田雖義旗不竟終厥亦足以見人心之所嚮矣降及近世眞理昌明民族民權益然人心加以虜氛不競强敵四臨不賓我土宇以其鄰國人雖不肖猶是神明之胄安能忍此終古以忝先人之靈乎於是仗

(0357)

臨時政府公報　紀事　第十七號　七

大总统谒陵文

President Sun Yat-sen's Funeral Oration Delivered at the Ming Tomb

1912年2月15日，孙中山与文武官员在明孝陵谒陵

Dr. Sun Yat-sen with the civil officials and military officers paid homage at the Ming Tomb on 15 February 1912.

1912年3月底，北方议和代表、北洋总理唐绍仪南下来到总统府。孙中山介绍唐绍仪加入同盟会。图为二人在总统办公室前合影

Dr. Sun Yat-sen introduced Tang Shaoyi, the Premier of the Beiyang Government to join the China Federal Association at the end of March 1912. Picture shows Dr. Sun Yat-sen posing with Tang Shaoyi in front of his office.

孙中山与唐绍仪、胡汉民等在秘书处前合影

President Sun Yat-sen Posing for a Group Photo with Tang Shaoyi and Hu Hanmin et al. in front of the Secretariat of the Nanjing Provisional Government

总统府秘书处（今摄）

Secretariat of the Nanjing Provisional Government (Picture taken in the 2010s)

解职前的孙中山

Dr. Sun Yat-sen before the Resignation of the Presidency

孙中山、唐绍仪与总统府军政人员合影

President Sun Yat-sen Posing for a Group Photo with Tang Shaoyi and Politic and Military Officers of the Provisional Government

1912 年 3 月，孙中山为粤军烈士墓题写的碑文

President Sun Yat-sen's Inscription to Honour the Guangdong Army Martyrs Before His Resignation

1912 年 3 月 5 日，孙中山出席追悼粤中倡义死难诸烈士大会

President Sun Yat-sen attended the ceremony of memorial service in honour of the Guangdong Army martyrs on 5 March 1912.

临时政府颁发的奖章（牌）、纪念章（牌）及发行的纪年币

Medals, Badges and Coins Issued by the Nanjing Provisional Government

1912年4月3日，军队在总统府列队送别孙中山离开南京

The Nanjing Provisional Government's troops lined up to see Dr. Sun Yat-sen off on 3 April 1912.

1912年4月3日，孙中山乘车离开总统府

Dr. Sun Yat-sen left the Nanjing Provisional Government by car on 3 April 1912.

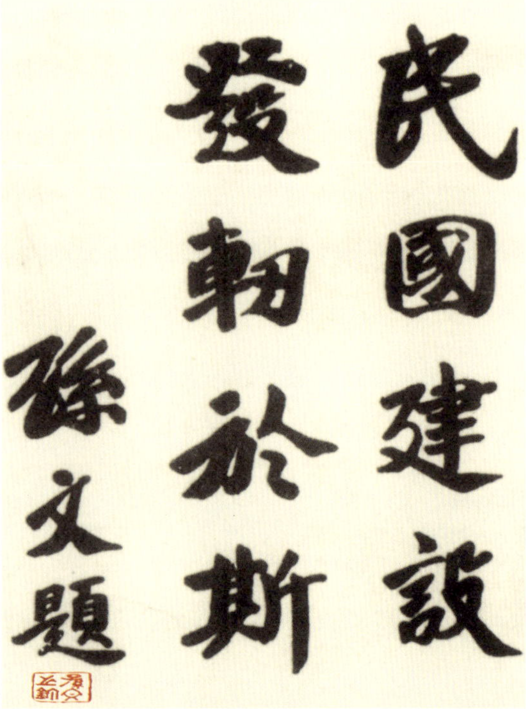

孙中山辞职后，致力于实业救国。这是孙中山的部分题词

Dr. Sun Yat-sen paid special attention to saving China with industry after his resignation. Picture shows some of his inscriptions.

孙中山解职后在上海与家人、友人合影

Dr. Sun Yat-sen Posing for a Group Photo with His Family Members and Friends in Shanghai after His Resignation

共和肇始（油画）

Initiation of the Republic (Oil Painting)

四

讨袁受挫 北洋政权频更迭

IV. Beiyang Regime Alternated Frequently after the Failure of the Second Revolution Anti-Yuan Shih-kai

1912 年 4 月，北洋政府任命黄兴为南京留守府留守。6 月，江苏都督府由苏州移驻南京，直至 1913 年 7 月“二次革命”反袁兵败。9 月，张勋率军攻陷南京。之后十多年，各路军阀纷纷在此角逐，这里先后成为江苏都督府、将军府、督军署，中华民国副总统府，江苏督办公署，五省联军总司令部，直鲁联军联合办事处等机构。政权频繁更迭，主官屡屡易人，政局更加动荡。

In April 1912, Yuan Shih-kai, the Second Provisional President appointed Huang Xing the Nanjing Resident-General. The Jiangsu Military Governor's Official Residence moved to Nanjing from Suzhou in June 1912. The Second Revolution against Yuan Shih-kai failed in July 1913. Zhang Xun's “Pigtail Troops” occupied Nanjing in September 1913. In following decade, warlords fought against one another for the control of Nanjing. The Presidential Palace kept changing hands between warlords. Several local governments and other organizations took it over, such as the Jiangsu Military Governor's Official Residence, the Vice-President Feng Guozhang's Office, the Jiangsu Pacification Commissioner's Office, Headquarters of Five-Province Allied Troops, and the Office of Zhili-Shandong Allied Army, etc. Regimes frequently changed, causing a turbulent political situation in this period.

南京留守府大堂

The Hall of the First Row of Houses of the Nanjing Resident-General

南京留守府留守黄兴

Huang Xing in the Nanjing Resident-General's Office

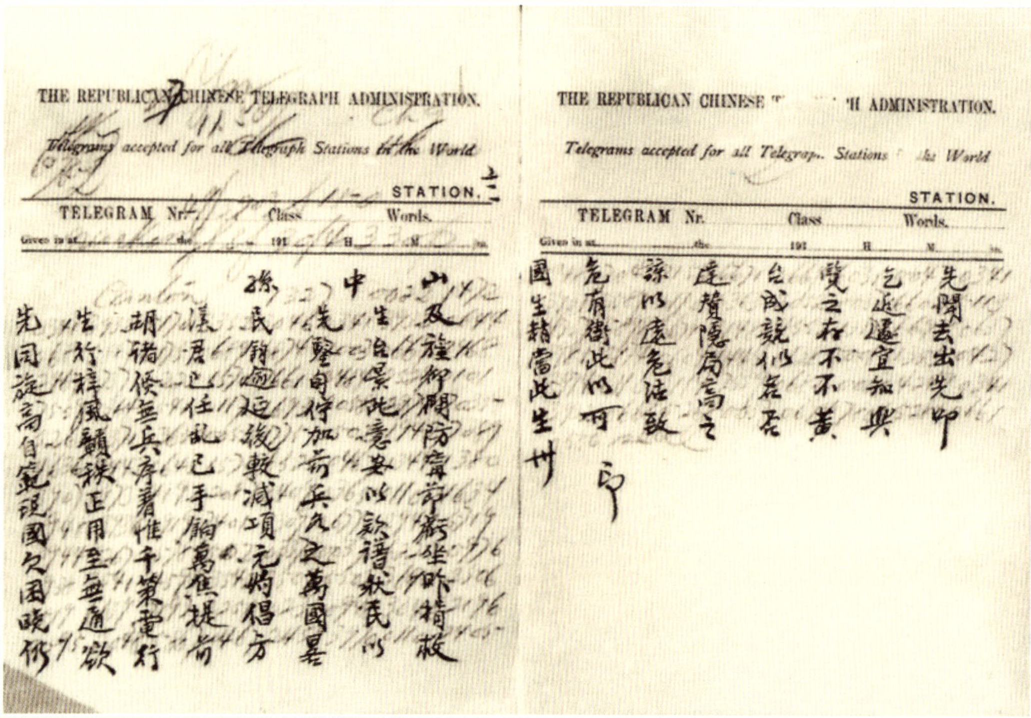

黄兴任留守期间给孙中山的电报，告知南京的军事动态

Huang Xing's Telegrams to Dr. Sun Yat-sen Reporting on the Military Situation in Nanjing

黄兴印章及南京留守府关防

Huang Xing's Private Seal and Official Seal of the Resident-General's Office

黄兴及留守府官兵在大堂合影

Huang Xing Posing for a Group Photo with Officers and Men of the Nanjing Resident–General's Office

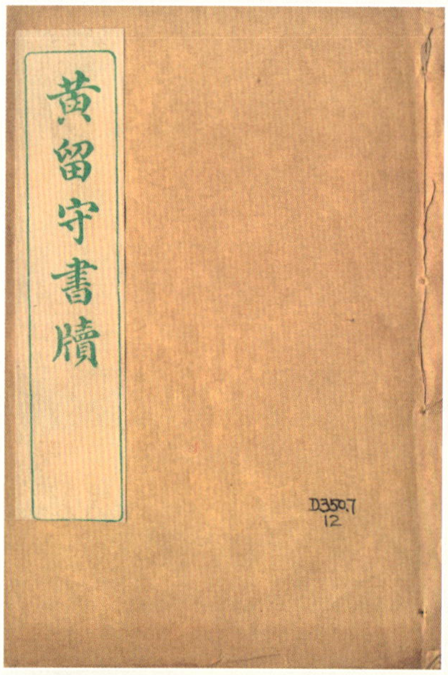

曾天飛等請設宣講所提倡國民捐由稟悉。該生等擬分設支部。將民國提倡國民捐意旨。預備宣講。以開民智。足見愛國熱心。深堪嘉尚。仰卽聯合同志。實力進行。藉紓國困。所請以王繩玉爲太倉支部理事及立案。着無庸議。

安慰軍民示

照得本留守因南方軍隊佈置漸將就緒。是以電請袁大總統將留守府撤銷。現値交替之際。本留守在任一日。必擔一日責任。非事事交卸清楚。接代有人。本留守決不忍拋棄我軍民也。切勿妄信浮言。自滋紛擾。切切特示。

解職敬告諸將士文

中華民國元年六月十四日。解職南京留守黄興。敬告我將士諸君左右。興承乏留守。已兩月矣。棉薄之材。處嫌疑之地。夙夜祇懼。幸賴諸君子一德一心。共扶危局。旣紉公誼。共鑒私衷。慨自南北統一。政府北遷。日月重光。鋒烟已靖。然戰爭之餘。四民失業。瘡痍滿目。雞犬時驚。差幸兩月來。商集於廛。士安於校。巳漸蘇積困。頓復舊觀。

黄留守書牘 卷下 二十一

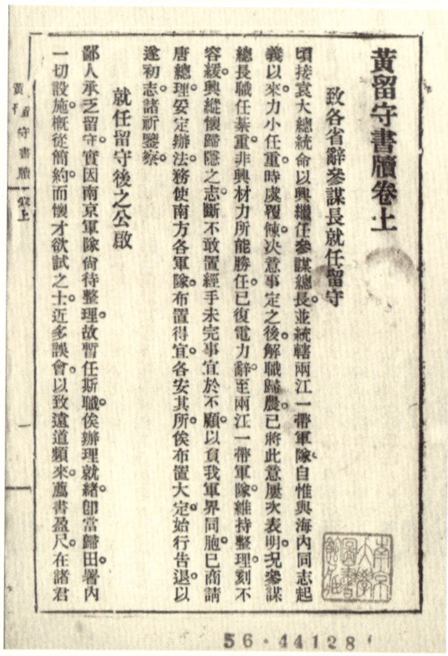

黄留守書牘卷上

致各省辭參謀長就任留守

頃接袁大總統命。以興繼任參謀總長。並統轄兩江一帶軍隊。自惟興海內同志起義以來。力小任重。時虞覆餗。決意事定之後。解職歸農。已將此意屢次表明。況參謀總長職任綦重。非興材力所能勝任。已復電力辭。至兩江一帶軍隊。維持整理。刻不容緩。興縱懷歸隱之志。斷不敢置經手未完事宜於不顧。以負我軍界同胞。已商請唐總理妥定辦法。務使南方各軍隊布置得宜。各安其所。俟布置大定。始行告退。以遂初志。諸祈鑒察。

就任留守後之公啟

鄙人承乏留守。實因南京軍隊尚待整理。故暫任斯職。俟辦理就緒。卽當歸田。署內一切設施。槪從簡約。而懷才欲試之士。近多誤會。以致遠道頻來。薦書盈尺。在諸君

黄留守書牘 卷上

《黄留守书牍》文本

Nanjing Resident–General Huang Xing's Written Messages

黄兴与家人合影

Huang Xing Posing for a Group Photo with His Family Members

黄兴夫人徐宗汉与留守府军人合影

Huang Xing's Wife Xu Zonghan Posing for a Group Photo with Military Officers in the Resident-General's Office

江苏都督程德全

Cheng Dequan, Jiangsu Military Governor

江苏代理都督庄蕴宽

Zhuang Yunkuan, Acting Jiangsu Military Governor

1912 年 10 月 10 日，江苏都督府在大堂前举行辛亥革命一周年纪念活动

Anniversary celebration of the 1911 Revolution was held in front of the hall of the first row houses of the Jiangsu Military Governor's Office on 10 October 1912.

1913年，江苏都督程德全（右二）与北洋总理熊希龄（右三）等在督府西花园石舫

Cheng Dequan (second from right) posed for a group photo with Xiong Xiling (third from right), Premier of the Beiyang Government, and others on the Stone Boat in 1913.

1913 年任江苏讨袁军总司令的黄兴

Huang Xing, Commander-in-Chief of the Jiangsu Anti-Yuan (Shih-kai) Army in the Second Revolution in 1913

黄兴（中）在督府西花园假山

Huang Xing (center) Posing with His Officers in Front of Rockery in the West Garden

讨袁军炮兵

The Artillery Troops of the Anti-Yuan (Shih-kai) Army in the Second Revolution in 1913

江苏代都督兼讨袁军总司令章梓

Zhang Zi, Acting Jiangsu Military Governor and Concurrently the Commander of the Anti-Yuan (Shih-kai) Army in the Second Revolution in 1913

数度占领都督府、自封为讨袁军临时总司令的何海鸣

He Haiming, proclaimed himself Provisional Commander-in-Chief of the Anti-Yuan Army, led troops to occupy the Jiangsu Military Governor's Office three times in 1913.

何海鸣（图正中者）与讨袁军官兵合影

He Haiming (center) Posing for a Group Photo with Officers and Men of the Anti-Yuan Army

“辫帅”张勋

Zhang Xun, Commander-in-Chief of the “Pigtail Army”

攻破南京城的辫军

Zhang Xun's “Pigtail Army” after the Occupation of Nanjing

1916 年，冯国璋任副总统时佩戴的纪念章（正反面）

Commemorative Badge on Feng Guozhang's Taking Vice-President of the Beiyang Government

1913 年 12 月至 1917 年 8 月，先后任江苏都督、江苏将军、江苏督军、中华民国副总统的冯国璋

Feng Guozhang, Jiangsu Military Governor from December 1913 to October 1916 and Vice-President of the Beiyang Government in August 1917

冯国璋任上所建的西式平房（今摄）

One-storey Western style House Built by Feng Guozhang (Picture taken in the 2010s)

1917 年 7 月任江苏督军的齐耀琳

Qi Yaolin, Jiangsu Military Governor in July 1917

1917 年 8 月至 1920 年 10 月任江苏督军的李纯

Li Chun, Jiangsu Military Governor from August 1917 to October 1920

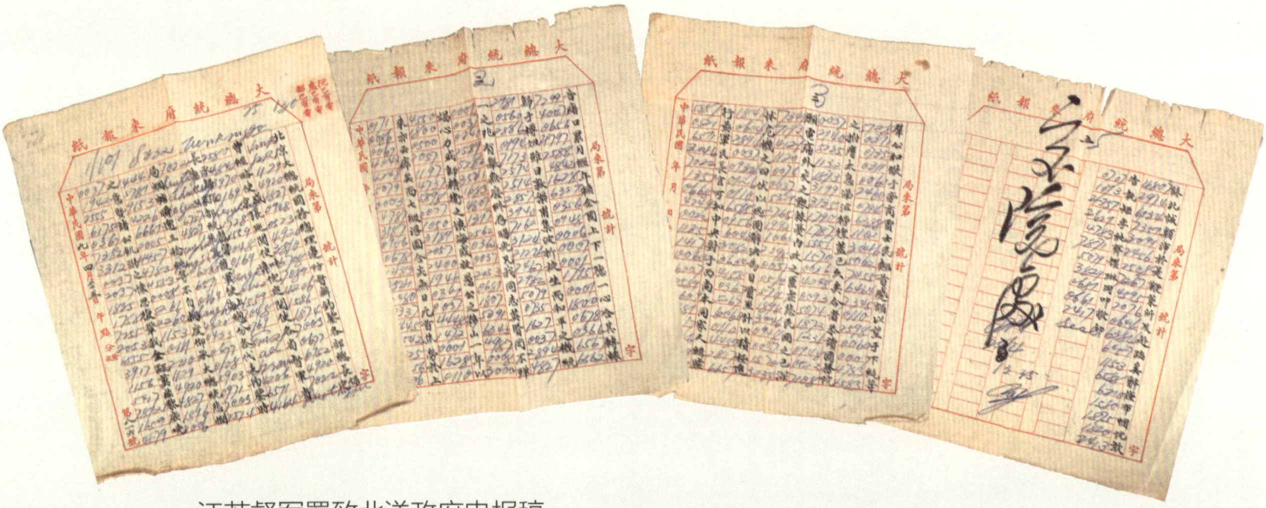

江苏督军署致北洋政府电报稿

Telegram from the Jiangsu Military Governor's Office to the Beiyang Government

1924 年 12 月至 1925 年 1 月

任江苏代理督办的韩国钧

Han Guojun, Acting Jiangsu Military Governor from December 1924 to January 1925

1920 年 10 月至 1924 年 12 月

任江苏督军的齐燮元

Qi Xieyuan, Jiangsu Military Governor from October 1920 to December 1924

1925 年 8 月至 11 月任江苏军务督办的杨宇霆

Yang Yuting, Superintendent of Jiangsu Military Affairs from August to November 1925

1925 年 1 月至 8 月任江浙宣抚使的卢永祥

Lu Yongxiang, Jiangsu–Zhejiang Pacification Commissioner from January to August 1925

1925 年 8 月兼任江苏军务督办的郑谦

Zheng Qian, Concurrently the Superintendent of the Jiangsu Military Affairs in August 1925

1927 年 3 月任直鲁联军联合办事处主任的张宗昌

Zhang Zongchang, Director of the Joint Office of the Zhili–Shandong Allied Troops in March 1927

1925 年 11 月任江苏军务督办、后任五省联军总司令的孙传芳

Sun Chuanfang, Superintendent of Jiangsu Military Affairs in November 1925, and Then Commander–in–Chief of Five–Province Allied Troops

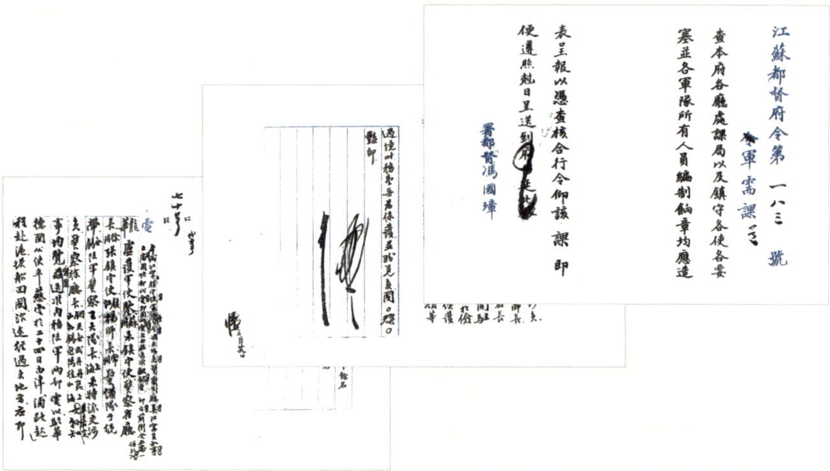

江蘇都督府令第 一八三 號
令軍需課
查本府各廳處課局以及鎮守各使各要
塞並各軍隊所有人員編制餉章均應造
表呈報以憑查核合行令仰該 課 即
便遵照剋日呈送
署都督馮國璋

江苏都督府令文本

Order of the Jiangsu Military Governor's Office

署江蘇都督馮

一件 咨復陸軍部前在第二軍及江淮宣撫使任內預支各款礙難稟送收據情形由

軍需課主辦第 號

七月 日

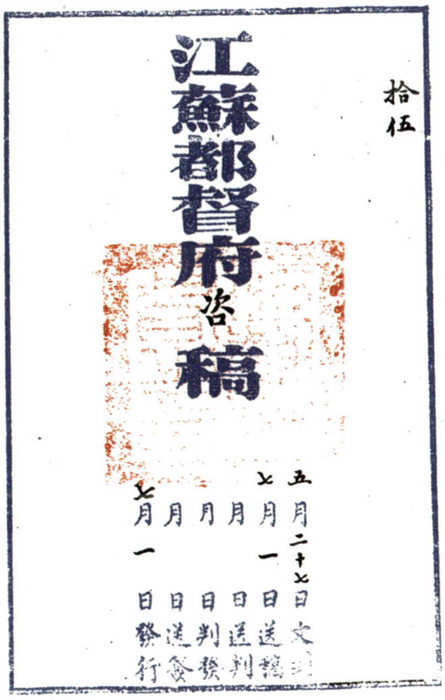

江蘇都督府咨稿

拾伍

五月二十七日文到

七月 日送稿

月 日送判

月 日判發

月 日送簽

七月一日發行

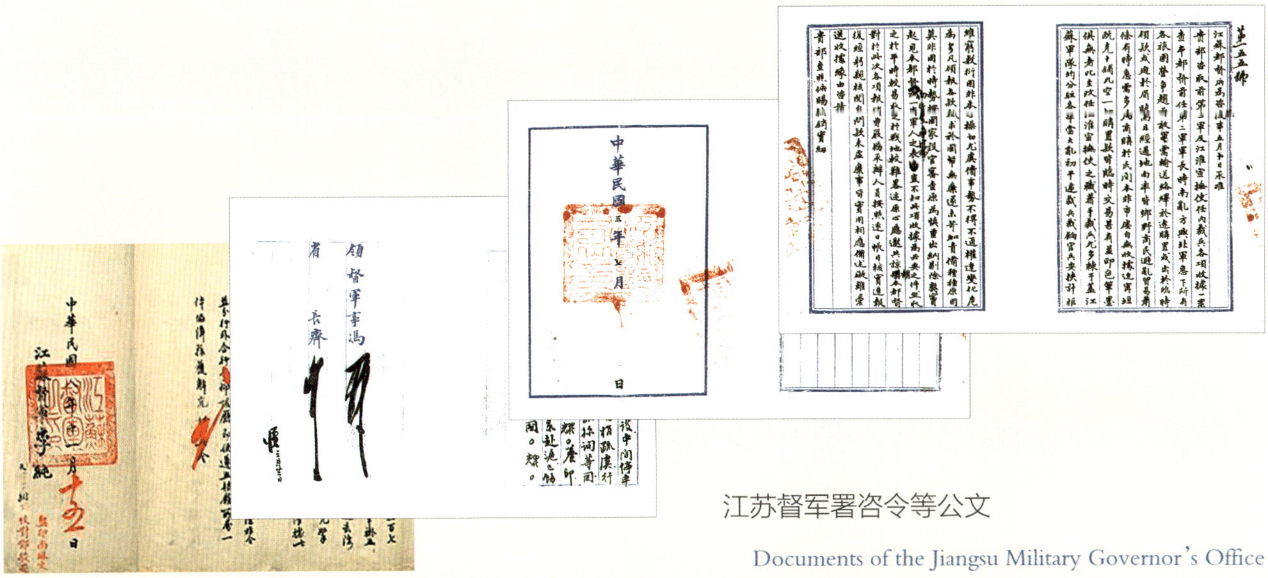

江苏督军署咨令等公文

Documents of the Jiangsu Military Governor's Office

北洋军在督署北校场操练

The Beiyang Forces Drilling in Drill Ground

五

国府奠都　枢府春秋十年路

V. Nationalist Government Making Nanjing Its Capital and Staying Here for Ten Years

1927年4月18日，国民政府在原中华民国临时参议院成立，9月底移驻原江苏督军署办公。国民革命军总司令部与北伐军总司令部曾在西花园合署办公。国民政府初设四常委，至1928年改组后，谭延闿、蒋介石、林森先后任国民政府主席。国民政府"五院制"架构建立后，辟国府东院为行政院。

九一八事变后，日军侵华日急，国内要求政府出兵抗日的呼声日益高涨。因淞沪战争爆发，国民政府曾于1932年和1937年两度"迁都"洛阳和重庆。

The Nationalist Government was established in the former Senate of the Nanjing Provisional Government on 18 April 1927 and moved to the former Jiangsu Military Governor's Official Residence at the end of September 1927. There were four members of the Standing Committee of the Nationalist Government in its early days. Tan Yankai, Chiang Kai-shek and Lin Sen successively took up the post of Chairman of it after its reform of 1928. The Nationalist Government was reformed into "Five-Yuan". The Executive Yuan used the East Garden of the compound of the Nationalist Government as its seat.

1927 年 4 月 18 日，国民政府在原中华民国临时参议院成立。图为成立典礼合影

The Nationalist Government was established in the former Senate of the Nanjing Provisional Government on 18 April 1927. A Group Photo taken after the Celebration of the Establishment of the Nationalist Government.

“中华民国之玺”印文

The Seal of the Republic of China

“中华民国国民政府印”印文

The Seal of the Nationalist Government of the Republic of China

设于原中华民国临时参议院的国民政府，1927 年 9 月 20 日迁原督军署办公

The gate of the Nationalist Government in the former Senate of the Nanjing Provisional Government, the Government moved to the former Jiangsu Military Governor's Official Residence on 20 September 1927.

国民政府常委胡汉民

Standing Committee Member Hu Hanmin of the Nationalist Government

国民政府常委伍朝枢

Standing Committee Member Wu Chaoshu of the Nationalist Government

簡任狀

簡字第貳貳號

任命皮宗石為中央法制委員會委員此狀

常務委員 胡漢民 古應芬 伍朝樞 張人傑

中華民國十六年八月五日

国民政府成立之初，实行常委制（先为四人，后增至七人）。这是四常委签署的简任状

Certificate of Appointment Signed by the Four Standing Committee Members

国民政府常委古应芬

Standing Committee Member Gu Yingfen of the Nationalist Government

国民政府常委张人杰

Standing Committee Member Zhang Renjie of the Nationalist Government

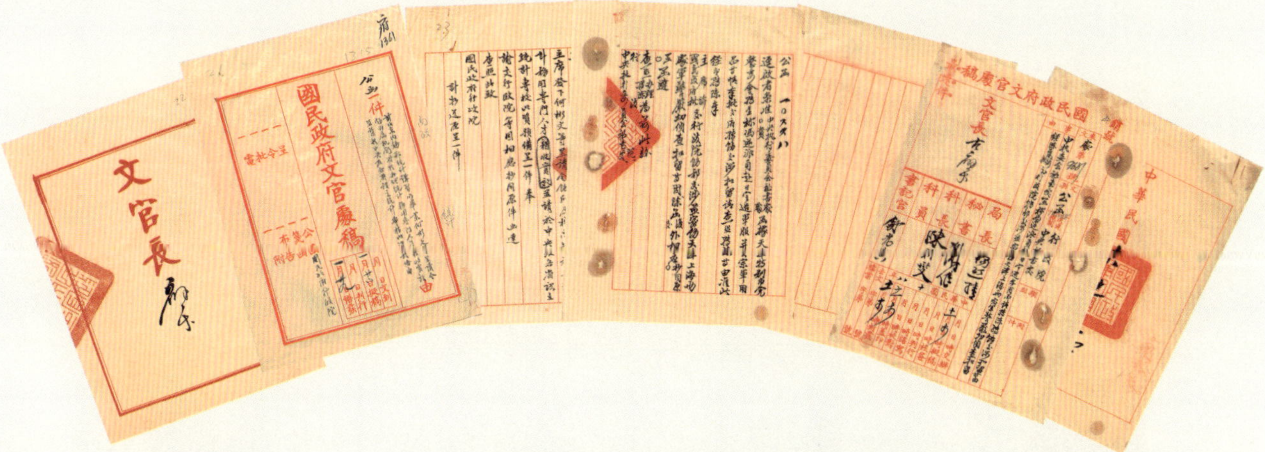

国民政府文官处致行政院、国民党中央执行委员会秘书处公函稿

Message from the Civil Service of the Nationalist Government to the Executive Yuan and the Central Executive Committee of the KMT

1928年2月至10月任国民政府首任主席的谭延闿。谭擅长书法

Tan Yankai, who was good at calligraphy, took office of the first Chairman of the Nationalist Government from February to October 1928.

谭延闿的书法

Calligraphy of Tan Yankai

伍朝枢、谭延闿（中）、孙科合影

Tan Yankai (center) Posing a Photo with Wu Chaoshu and Sun Fo

谭延闿（前排右三）在国民政府主席任上的合影

Chairman Tan Yankai Posing with Others

1928 年 10 月蒋介石任国府主席后，与夫人宋美龄在国民政府首次接见外宾（丹麦太子夫妇）

Chiang Kai-shek and Song Meiling received foreign guests (Prince of Denmark and his wife) for the first time after he became Chairman of the Nationalist Government in October 1928.

1928 年 10 月至 1931 年 12 月任国民政府主席的蒋介石，集党政军大权于一身

Chiang Kai-shek, who wielded the powers of party, government and military, took office of the second Chairman of the Nationalist Government from October 1928 to December 1931.

门楼匾额“国民政府”四字由谭延闿所书（一说为其弟谭泽闿书），门楼顶部的旗杆基座为复式造型，形同官帽

There was a horizontal inscribed board with four Chinese characters: “Guo Min Zheng Fu” above the gate of the Nationalist Government, which was Tan Yankai’s calligraphy (It is also said that it is his younger brother Tan Zekai’s calligraphy).

1929 年 12 月落成的国民政府大门门楼，由建筑师姚彬设计绘图，文达工程建筑公司中标承建。总造价为 2.9455 万元大洋。新建的大门是典型的西方古典门廊式建筑，朝南立面的外部采用八根古希腊爱奥尼柱式构图，门楼顶部平台东西北三面为镂空女儿墙，三堂拱形门外圆内方，含有诸多中国元素

The gate tower of the Nationalist Government was built in December 1929. It was designed by Yao Bin and built by the Wenda Engineering and Construction Co.. It cost a total of 29455 dollars. The gate is a typical structure of Western classical portico-pattern. It faces south with eight beautiful, Ionic columns in front of it in the style of Ancient Greece. There are three arched entrances opening into the inner side of the gate. There are three square doors on the inner side of the gate, which have a lot of Chinese elements.

1931年12月，林森代理国民政府主席，于1932年1月1日正式就任，连任至1943年。《国民政府组织法》规定，“国民政府主席不负实际责任”

Lin Sen took up the post of Acting Chairman from December 1931, and was elected as Chairman on 1 January 1932 and served consecutive terms to 1943.

林森在读书

Lin Sen is reading.

1932 年 1 月 1 日林森就任国民政府主席后，在国府大堂与五院院长及党政军要员合影

Chairman Lin Sen posed for a group photo with the Presidents of the "Five-Yuan" and important party, government and military officials on 1 January 1932.

為完全自由行使職權

國府移駐洛陽辦公

望軍政長官同心協力各盡所職

全國民衆須勇毅沉着共赴國難

務使暴力無所施正義得以申

政府要人赴洛陽主持

何應欽維持首都治安

羅文幹留京主持外交

英美對滬

1932年1月28日，淞沪战争爆发。这是《中央日报》关于国民政府“移驻”洛阳的报道

Reports on After the Outbreak of the Song-Hu Anti-Japanese Campaign, the Nationalist Government moved to Luoyang , Henan province.

1932 年 1 月底，林森率国民政府离开南京“移驻”洛阳。同年 12 月 1 日返回南京

The Nationalist Government headed by Lin Sen moved to Luoyang from Nanjing at the end of January 1932 and returned back on 1 December 1932.

西迁洛阳时的国民政府大门

Gate of the Nationalist Government Before Moving to Luoyang

1928年10月21日，国民政府司法院正副院长暨文官长、参军长、各局长就职宣誓典礼合影

President and Vice President of the Judicial Yuan and other officials took a group photo after the inauguration on 21 October 1928.

国民政府训练总监部全体职员在国民政府大礼堂就职合影

The Officers of the Department of Military Training took a group photo after the inauguration.

1928年10月25日，国民政府行政院正副院长暨各部部长在国府大礼堂就职典礼合影

President and Vice President of Executive Yuan and Ministers took a group photo after the inauguration on 25 October 1928.

1929年10月10日，国府主席阅兵典礼合影。前排左起蒋介石、谭延闿、胡汉民、林森、戴季陶、赵戴文

Picture shows the military review of the Nationalist Government's Chairman on 10 October 1929.

1930年1月1日，国民政府元旦合影

Picture shows the celebration of New Year's Day of 1930 by the Nationalist Government.

1929 年 12 月，蒋介石在国民政府召开“国军编遣会议”。图为会议代表在煦园合影

Representatives Attending the Conference of Reorganizing National Revolutionary Army Presided over by Chiang Kai-shek in December 1929

大堂暖阁（今摄）

The Warm Pavilion of the First Row of Houses (Picture taken in the 2010s)

1931 年 4 月，国民政府主计长兼岁计局长陈其采（前立者）及各主计官，岁计、会计、统计局各局长等，在国府大礼堂宣誓就职

The Inauguration of Chen Qicai (standing in front), Comptroller General and Concurrently Director of Annual Counting Office, and Other Accounting Officials in April 1931

1934年2月，九世班禅（左二）就任国府委员时与国府主席林森等人在国府大堂合影

Chairman Lin Sen posed for a group photo with Panchen (second from left) who took the office of a member of the Nationalist Government in February 1934.

1935年8月1日，孔颜孟曾四圣奉祀官在国府就职时合影

The Inauguration of Officials for Offering Sacrifices to Confucius, and Other Three Sages on 1 August 1935

国府主席林森在国民政府册封安钦呼图克图（右三）典礼上的合影

Lin Sen in the Ceremony Granting the Title of "Hutuketu" to Living Buddha An Qin (third from right) by the Nationalist Government

1931 年 1 月 19 日，国府警卫师师长、副师长、旅长就职典礼合影

The Inauguration of Commander and Deputy Commander of Division of Guards and Others on 19 January 1931

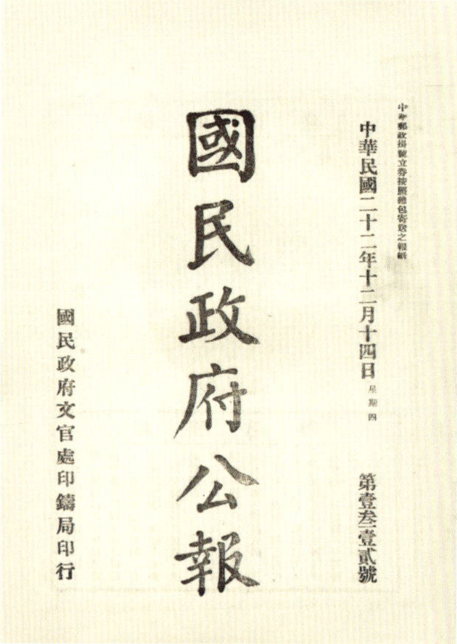

中華郵政掛號立券按照總包寄遞之報紙

中華民國二十二年十二月十四日 星期四

國民政府公報

第壹叁壹貳號

國民政府文官處印鑄局印行

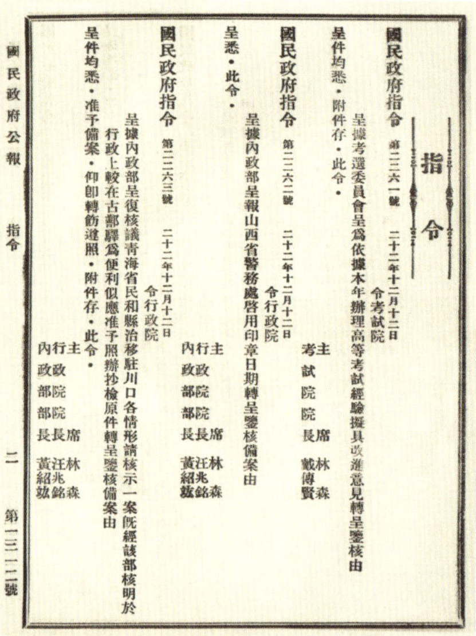

指令

國民政府指令 第二三六一號 二十二年十二月十二日

令考試院

呈據考選委員會呈爲依據本年辦理高等考試經驗擬具改進意見轉呈鑒核由

呈件均悉・附件存・此令・

主席 林森

考試院院長 戴傳賢

國民政府指令 第二三六二號 二十二年十二月十二日

令行政院

呈據內政部呈報山西省警務處啓用印章日期轉呈鑒核備案由

呈悉・此令・

主席 林森

行政院院長 汪兆銘

內政部部長 黃紹竑

國民政府指令 第二三六三號 二十二年十二月十二日

令行政院

呈據內政部呈復核議青海省民和縣治移駐川口各情形請核示一案既經該部核明於行政上較在古鄯驛爲便利似應准予照辦抄檢原件轉呈鑒核備案由

呈件均悉・准予備案・仰卽轉飭遵照・附件存・此令・

主席 林森

行政院院長 汪兆銘

內政部部長 黃紹竑

國民政府公報 指令 二 第一三一二號

《国民政府公报》文本

Gazette of the Nationalist Government

1934 年 12 月，中央监委委员兼陆海空军副司令张学良抵南京

Zhang Xueliang, member of the Central Committee of Supervision, met with well-wishers in the compound of the Nationalist Government in December 1934.

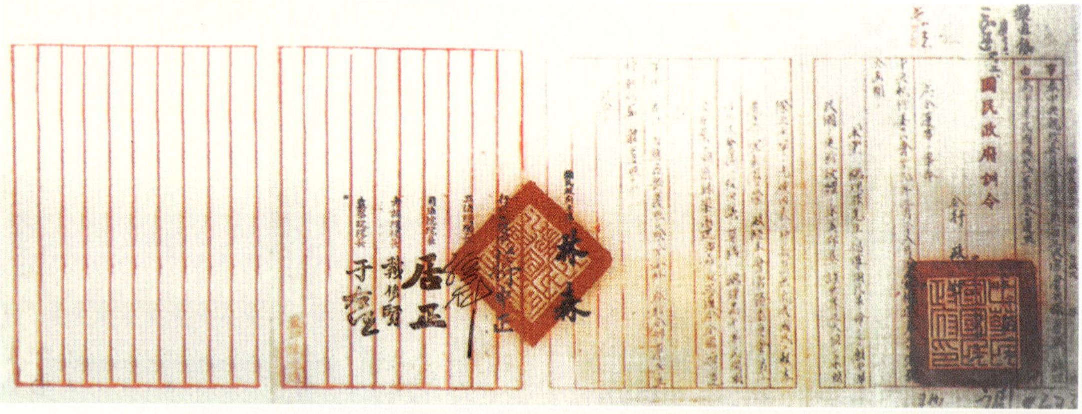

1936 年 11 月 12 日，在国民政府礼堂举行的“总理纪念周”上，林森率五院院长签署尊称孙中山为“国父”的国民政府训令

The Nationalist Government’s order signed by Lin Sen and Presidents of “Five-Yuan”, in which Sun Yat-sen was honoured as the “Founding Father” in the “Dr. Sun Yat-sen Memorial Week” on 12 November 1936.

1937年1月1日，国民政府在大礼堂举行授勋仪式

The Nationalist Government held a ceremony conferring order at the Grand Hall on 1 January 1937.

1937年1月，国民政府及行政院举行餐会，林森主持，汪精卫讲话。会议讨论中日濒临全面战争的问题

Nationalist Government held a dinner party discussing on the verge of all-out war between China and Japan in January 1937.

1931年冬，李济深（左）与吴稚晖在国府合影

Li Jishen (left) posed for a photo with Wu Zhihui in the winter of 1931.

1932年1月1日国民政府主席与五院院长就职后，立法院院长孙科接受官员道贺

Sun Fo, President of Legislation Yuan accepted congratulations from officials after the inauguration of the Chairman of the Nationalist Government and other presidents on 1 January 1932.

1932年1月，新任外交部部长陈友仁与夫人在国民政府院内留影

Eugene Chen, Newly Foreign Affairs Minister, and his wife took a photo in the compound of the Nationalist Government in January 1932.

1934年1月1日，唐生智、陈调元就任训练总监和军事参议院院长后合影。右起唐生智、朱培德、何应钦、陈调元、张治中

Photo Taken after the Inauguration of Tang Shengzhi, Chief of the Department of Military Training, and Chen Diaoyuan, President of Military Advisory Council on 1 January 1934

1931 年 11 月 26 日，京沪平杭学生在国府门前示威，要求政府出兵抗日

Students from Nanjing, Shanghai, Beiping and Hangzhou held a demonstration in front of the Nationalist Government and asked the government to fight against Japan on 26 November 1931.

1931 年 12 月，上海学生来南京请愿，要求政府出兵抗日。学生们在国民政府院内静坐，等待蒋介石出来答复

Students from Shanghai waited in the compound of the Nationalist Government to present a petition to Chiang Kai-shek requesting that the Government fight against Japan in December 1931.

1931 年 12 月，监察院院长于右任在国民政府院内向请愿学生发表讲话

Yu Youren, President of the Control Yuan, made a speech to the petitioning students in December 1931.

1935 年 12 月，南京高校学生响应北平“一二·九”运动，在国府门前游行示威

Students from Nanjing universities held a demonstration to support the December Ninth Movement in front of the Nationalist Government in December 1935.

1932 年 3 月，李顿调查团来中国调查九一八事变真相。图为李顿率团在国民政府

The Lytton Commission came to China to conduct an enquiry into the September 18th Incident in March 1932.

蒋介石在国民政府宴请李顿调查团一行

Chiang Kai-shek hosted a banquet for the Lytton Commission in the Nationalist Government.

1931年9月21日，蒋介石与宋美龄在国民政府接见来江苏高邮救灾的美国飞行员林德伯格夫妇

Chiang Kai-shek and Soong Meiling received American pilot Lindbergh and his wife on 21 September 1931,who provided disaster relief in Gaoyou, Jiangsu.

1935年9月17日，美国大使詹森（左二）在国民政府递交国书后，与国府主席林森等合影

N. T. Johnson (second from left), American Ambassador to China, presented his credentials in the Nationalist Government on 17 September 1935.

国民政府摄影处（今摄）

Place where heads of the Nationalist Government used to took Photographs (Picture taken in the 2010s)

1933年3月6日，英国新任驻华公使开设递交国书后，步出国民政府礼堂

New British Minister to China stepped out of the Grand Hall of the Nationalist Government after presenting his credentials on 6 March 1933.

1933年5月2日，苏联大使鲍格莫洛夫（左二）在国府递交国书时与国民政府主席林森等合影

Lin Sen posed for a photo with D. Bogomolov (second from left), Soviet Ambassador to China, after Bogomolov presented his credentials on 2 May 1933.

1935 年 9 月 14 日，德国首任驻华大使陶德曼在国民政府呈递国书

O. P. Trautmann, the first German Ambassador to China presented his credentials in the Nationalist Government on 14 September 1935.

1936 年 5 月， 行政院院长蒋介石在国民政府会见日本大使川樾茂（右二）

Chiang Kai-shek, President of the Executive Yuan, received Shigeru Kawagoe (second from right), Japanese Ambassador to China in the Nationalist Government in May 1936.

1934 年，比利时王国专使纳尔逊在礼堂谒见国民政府主席林森

The Belgian King's envoy had an audience with Lin Sen, Chairman of the Nationalist Government in 1934.

礼堂内景（今摄）

Indoor Scene of the Grand Hall (Picture taken in the 2010s)

1936 年，外交部部长张群（中）以及王正廷（右），会见挪威公使高兰（左）

Zhang Qun, Minister of Foreign Affairs (center) and Wang Zhengting (right) received F. Koren, Norwegian Minister to China (left) in 1936.

国民政府主席林森（左三）在国府接见意大利驻华大使罗亚谷诺（右二）

Chairman Lin Sen Receiving the Italian Ambassador to China (second from right) in the Nationalist Government.

1934 年 1 月，前来南京参加国民党四中全会的九世班禅（前排中）与张群、丁惟汾等要员合影

Panchen posed for a group photo with Zhang Qun, Ding Weifen and other officials in January 1934.

1935 年 12 月落成的国民政府办公楼。系国民政府主席林森任上所建，林森字子超，故又称“子超楼”。该楼为国民政府的主体建筑，位于大院中轴线北端。由中央大学建筑系教授虞炳烈设计，鲁创营造厂承建，整个工程耗资 106952 元。该楼设计摒弃了传统的宫殿大屋顶式样，立面采用西式的建筑平面组合与立体构图，色调简洁明快，呈完全对称形，属典型的公共行政建筑，为中国新民族建筑的经典之作

The office building of the Nationalist Government was designed by Yu Binglie, professor of the Central University, and built by the Luchuang Engineering Factory, and completed in December 1935. It cast a total of 106952 dollars. It was also called “Zichao Building” because Lin Sen, Chairman of the Nationalist Government, styled himself “Zichao”. It was a typical of new ethnic building prevalent during that period.

子超楼（今摄）

“Zichao” Building (Picture taken in the 2010s)

林森为国民政府国务会议厅题写的匾额

A Horizontal Inscribed Board with Eight Chinese Characters Written by Lin Sen in the State Conference Hall of the Nationalist Government

国民政府东花园喷水池

Fountain in the Eastern Garden in the Compound of the Nationalist Government

东花园喷水池（今摄）

Fountain in the Eastern Garden in the Compound of the Nationalist Government (Picture taken in the 2010s)

国民政府礼堂，在大堂西暖阁原址所建。这是 1929 年改建后的礼堂

Grand Hall of the Nationalist Government was erected on the former site of the Warm Pavilion in 1929.

礼堂正门。“礼堂”二字由林森题写（今摄）

Grand Hall (Picture taken in the 2010s)

20世纪20年代国民政府鸟瞰图

Birds-Eye View of the Compound of the Nationalist Government in the 1920s

20世纪30年代国民政府俯瞰图

Birds-Eye View of the Compound of the Nationalist Government in the 1930s

1928 年 10 月，国民政府行政院成立，设在国府东院。图为 20 世纪 30 年代落成的行政院大门，“行政院”三字为谭延闿所书

The Executive Yuan was formed in the East Garden of the Nationalist Government in October 1928. Picture shows that the gate of the Executive Yuan was completed in the 1930s. The three Chinese characters “Xing Zheng Yuan” (i.e. the Executive Yuan) on the gate were written by Tan Yankai.

行政院大门（今摄）

Gate of the Executive Yuan (Picture taken in the 2010s)

国民政府行政院办公楼（北楼）

Office Building of the Executive Yuan (North Building)

原行政院办公楼（今摄）

Office Building of the Executive Yuan (Picture taken in the 2010s)

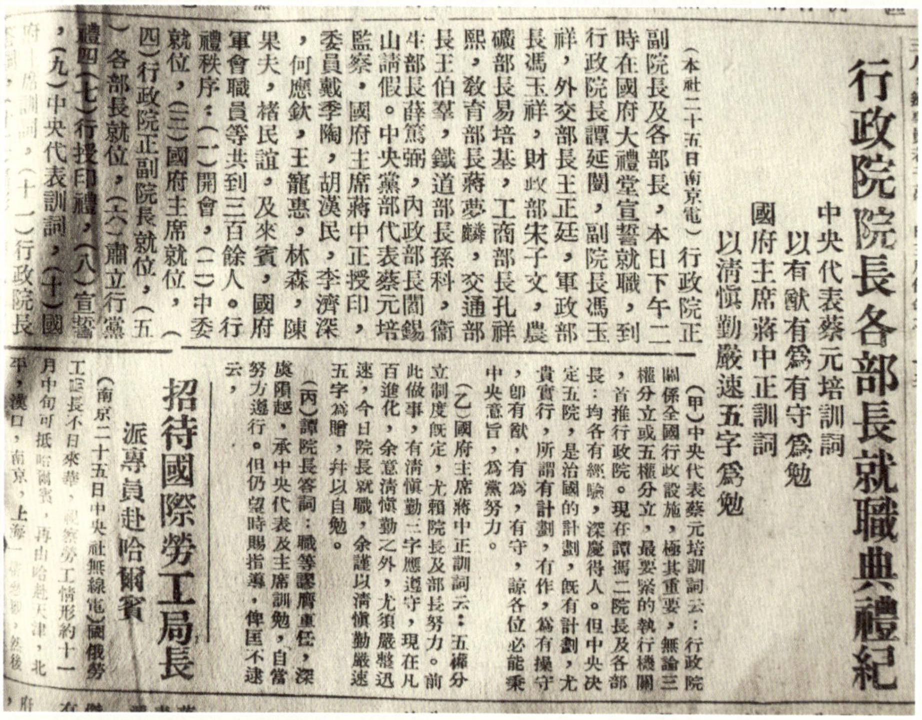

行政院院長各部長就職典禮紀

中央代表蔡元培訓詞 以有猷有為有守為勉
國府主席蔣中正訓詞 以清慎勤嚴速五字為勉

（本社二十五日南京電）行政院正副院長及各部長，本日下午二時在國府大禮堂宣誓就職，到行政院長譚延闓，副院長馮玉祥，外交部長王正廷，軍政部長馮玉祥，財政部宋子文，農礦部長易培基，工商部長孔祥熙，教育部長蔣夢麟，交通部長王伯羣，鐵道部長孫科，衛生部長薛篤弼，內政部長閻錫山請假。中央黨部代表蔡元培，監察，國府主席蔣中正授印，委員戴季陶，胡漢民，李濟深，何應欽，王寵惠，林森，陳果夫，褚民誼，及來賓，國府軍會職員等共到三百餘人。行禮秩序：（一）開會，（二）中委就位，（三）國府主席就位，（四）行政院正副院長就位，（五）各部長就位，（六）肅立行黨禮（七）行授印禮，（八）宣誓，（九）中央代表訓詞，（十）國府主席訓詞，（十一）行政院長

（甲）中央代表蔡元培訓詞云：行政院關係全國行政設施，極其重要，無論三權分立或五權分立，最要緊的執行機關，首推行政院。現在譚馮二院長及各部長：均各有經驗，深慶得人。但中央決定五院，是治國的計劃，既有計劃，尤貴實行，所謂有計劃，有作，為有操守，即有猷，有為，有守，諒各位必能秉中央意旨，為黨努力。

（乙）國府主席蔣中正訓詞云：五權分立制度既定，尤賴院長及部長努力。前此做事，有清慎勤三字應遵守，現在凡百進化，余意清慎勤之外，尤須嚴整迅速，今日院長就職，余謹以清慎勤嚴速五字為贈，并以自勉。

（丙）譚院長答詞：職等謬膺重任，深虞隕越，承中央代表及主席訓勉，自當努力遵行。但仍望時賜指導，俾匡不逮云，

招待國際勞工局長 派專員赴哈爾賓

（南京二十五日中央社無線電）國際勞工局長不日來華，視察勞工情形約十一月中旬可抵哈爾賓，再由哈赴天津，北平，漢口，南京，上海，一[illegible]，然後

1928 年 10 月 26 日《中央日报》关于行政院成立的报道

Report on the establishment of the Executive Yuan was carried by the Central Daily News on 26 October 1928.

1934 年 3 月 30 日，参加庚款机关联席会议第二次会议的人员在行政院新办公楼前合影

Participants of the 1900 Indemnity Joint Meeting posed for a group photo in front of the Office Building of the Executive Yuan on 30 March 1934.

行政院总办公厅

General Office of the Executive Yuan

行政院阅览室

Reading Room of the Executive Yuan

1934 年的行政院会议室

Meeting Room of the Executive Yuan in 1934

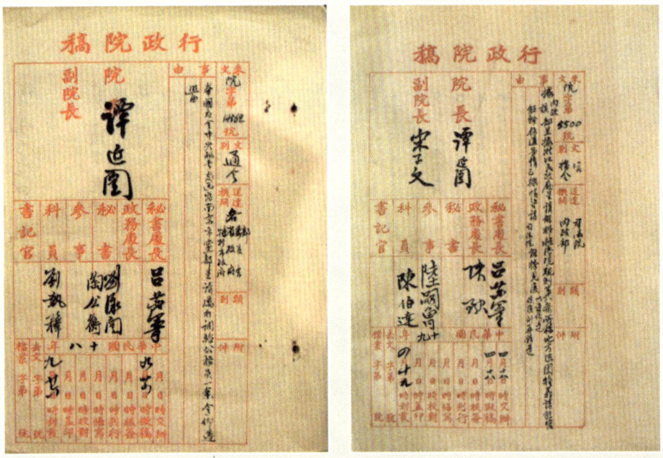

行政院档案

Files of the Executive Yuan

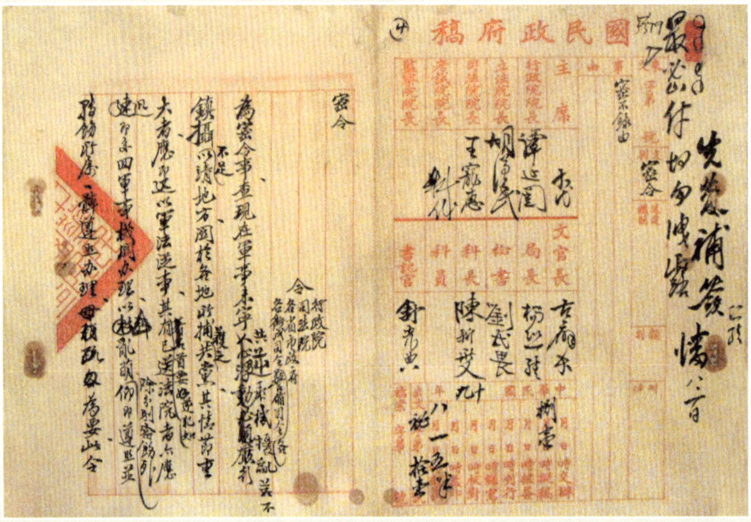

行政院为“五院”之首，这是“五院”公文稿

Draft Official Documents of the “Five-Yuan” of the Nationalist Government

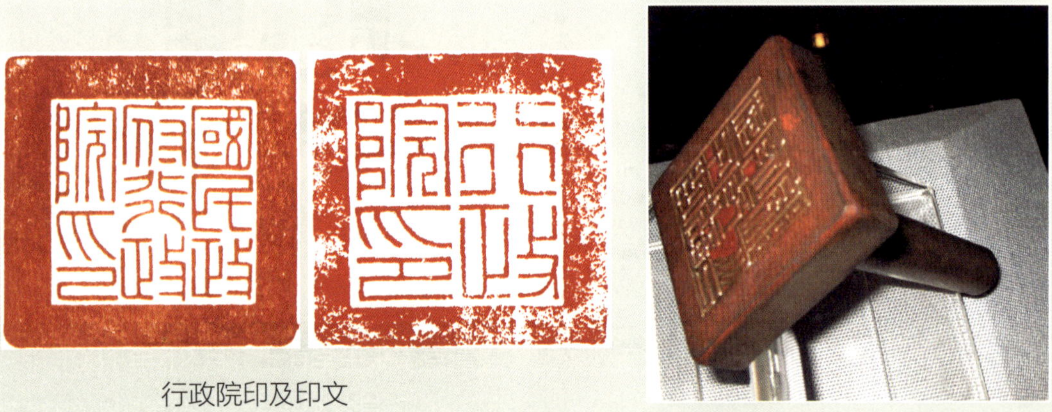

行政院印及印文

Seal of the Executive Yuan

国民政府立法院

Legislation Yuan of the Nationalist Government

国民政府司法院

Judicial Yuan of the Nationalist Government

国民政府监察院

Control Yuan of the Nationalist Government

国民政府考试院

Examination Yuan of the Nationalist Government

国民政府立法院印文

Seal of the Legislation Yuan

国民政府司法院印文

Seal of the Judicial Yuan

国民政府监察院印文

Seal of the Control Yuan

国民政府考试院印文

Seal of the Examination Yuan

1928 年国民政府实行“五院制”，其他四院相继成立

The Nationalist Government was formed into “Five-Yuan” in 1928 and the five yuans were successively set up.

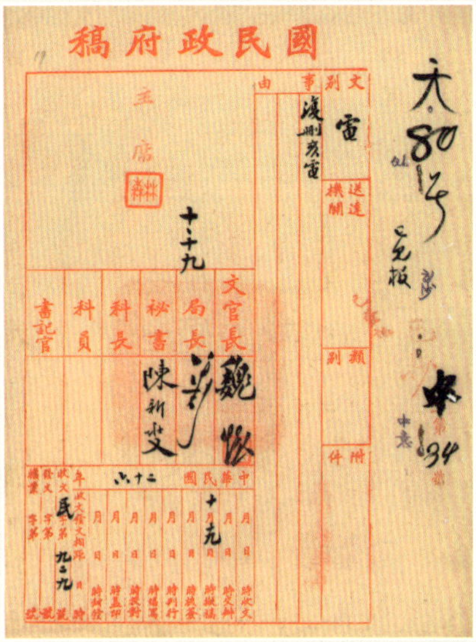

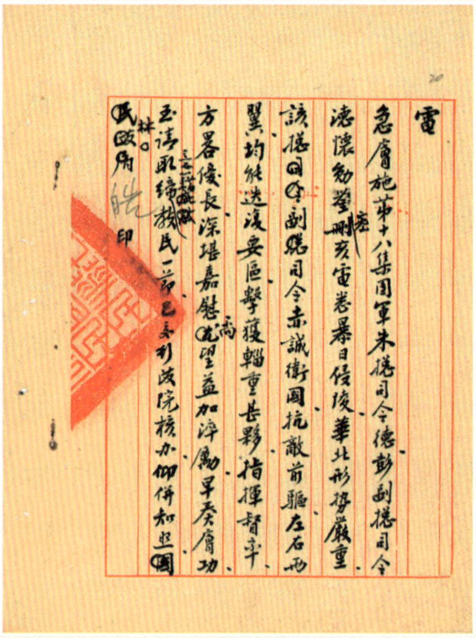

1937 年 10 月，林森签发的国民政府关于平型关大捷致朱德、彭德怀的复电，嘉勉第十八集团军将士“赤诚卫国，抗敌前驱”

Telegram Signed by Chairman Lin Sen to Zhu De and Peng Dehuai Concerning Praising and Encouraging the Officers and Men of the Eighteenth Group Army in October 1937

特授狀

特授蔣中正為陸海空軍大元帥統率全國陸海空軍此狀

國民政府主席 林森

1937 年 8 月第二次淞沪战争爆发后，林森签署的蒋介石为陆海空军大元帅的特授状

Especial Certificate of Appointment of Generalissimo Chiang Kai-shek Signed by Lin Sen in August 1937

抗战全面爆发后的国民政府大门

Gate of the Nationalist Government after the Lugou Bridge Incident in 1937

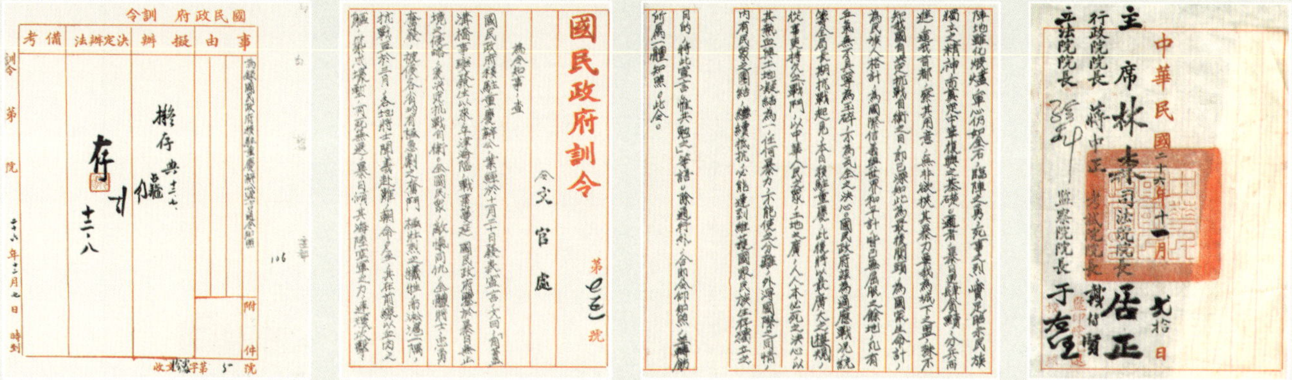

1937 年 11 月 20 日，国民政府主席及五院院长签署的“迁都”训令

Order Concerning the Move of Capital Signed by the Chairman of the Nationalist Government and the Presidents of Five-Yuan on 20 November 1937

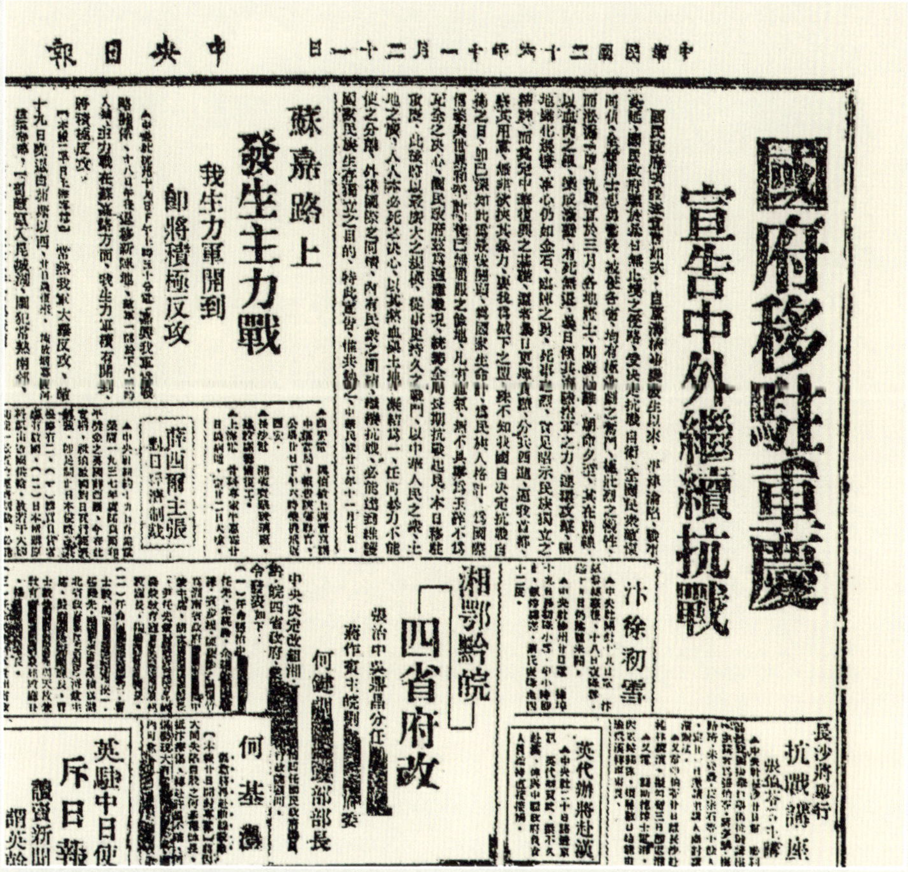
中央日報

中華民國二十六年十一月二十一日

國府移駐重慶
宣告中外繼續抗戰

蘇嘉路上發生主力戰
我生力軍開到 即將積極反攻

湘鄂黔皖四省府改

英駐日使斥日報

沐徐初雪

長沙將舉行抗戰講座

《中央日报》关于国民政府“移驻”重庆的报道

Report on the Nationalist Government’s move to Chongqing was carried by the Central Daily News on 21 November 1937.

国府西迁（油画）

Nationalist Government Moving to West (Oil Painting, by Shi Weiping)

六

南京沦陷　日伪张狂蒙国耻

VI. Occupation of Nanjing by Japanese Troops　The Chinese Nation Being Subject to Humiliation

1937年12月，南京沦陷。国民政府及行政院先后沦为日伪政权机关。侵华日军占领国民政府后，在此举行“入城式”，并以这里为第十六师团部(中岛部队)本部驻地。1938年3月，伪中华民国维新政府在此成立。1940年3月至1945年8月，这里先后成为汪伪政府立法院、考试院、监察院、铁道部、交通部、军事参议院等机关的办公处。

Nanjing was occupied by Japanese Troops in December 1937. The compound of the Nationalist Government served as the offices of Japanese and puppet organizations. They held the ceremony, marking their entry into Nanjing, in front of the gateway of the Nationalist Government and took the compound as the headquarters of the 16th Division of the Japanese Imperial Army. The so-called Reformed Government of the Republic of China was established in March 1938. It and the Executive Yuan under it used the compound as their seats. The Executive Yuan, Legislation Yuan, Examination Yuan, Control Yuan, Ministries of Communications and Railways and Military Advisory Council under Wang Jingwei's Government also used the compound as their seats from March 1940 to August 1945.

1937 年 12 月 13 日，南京沦陷。日军在国民政府门楼上升旗

Japanese Military Troops hoisted a flag on the gate tower of the Nationalist Government on 13 December 1937.

1937 年 12 月，日军占领国民政府，在大门上悬挂巨幅太阳旗，以炫耀武力

The gate tower of the Nationalist Government waved the Japanese red-sun flag in December 1937.

1937 年 12 月 17 日，侵华日军占领南京的“入城式”，以中山门为起点，向国民政府行进

Iwane Matsui entered into the Zhongshan Gate of Nanjing city on 17 December 1937.

侵华日军占领南京发行之邮政明信片——入城式

Postcard Showing the Ceremony Marking Their Entry into Nanjing Issued by Japanese Troops

侵华日军南京“入城式”的终点在国民政府

Japanese Troops Arriving at the gate of the Nationalist Government

侵华日军在国民政府大院举行"入城式",华中方面军司令官松井石根、上海派遣军司令朝香宫鸠彦、第十军司令柳川平助、海军第三舰队司令长谷川清粉墨登场

Iwane Matsui presided at the ceremony marking Japanese Troops' entry into Nanjing in the compound of the Nationalist Government.

日军南京"入城式"结束后,部分日军将领在国民政府院内广场举行"入城祭告式"

Some high-ranking officers of Japanese Troops prayed for themselves after their entry into Nanjing in the compound of the Nationalist Government.

1937 年圣诞节，日军中岛部队将国民政府占为兵营

Nakashima's Forces settled in the compound of the Nationalist Government on the Christmas Day of 1937.

南京沦陷后，日军在国民政府行政院大门前

Gate of the Executive Yuan of the Nationalist Government after the Occupation by Japanese Troops

国民政府沦于日军之手后，礼堂一片狼藉

Everything in the Hall of the Nationalist Government was scattered in disorder after the occupation by Japanese Troops.

日军将军用物资堆放在国民政府前院

Japanese military supplies were stacked in the courtyard of the Nationalist Government.

1938 年 3 月 28 日，日军在华中扶植的傀儡政权中华民国维新政府在原国民政府成立

The so-called Reformed Government of the Republic of China was established on 28 March.1938.

1938 年 10 月 10 日，伪维新政府官员与日军军官在原国民政府办公楼前合影

Officials of the so-called Reformed Government posed for a group photo with commanders of Japanese Aggressive Troops in front of the former office building of the Nationalist Government on 10 October 1938.

日酋山田在伪维新政府成立典礼上致辞

O. Yamada, Japanese Major General, Making a Congratulatory Speech in the Inaugural Ceremony of the so-called Reformed Government.

伪维新政府成立典礼结束后的合影

Photographs Taken after the Inaugural Ceremony

伪维新政府成立典礼结束后，伪府官员在原国民政府办公楼前合影

Officials of the so-called Reformed Government had their picture taken in front of the former office building of the Nationalist Government after the inauguration.

伪维新政府成立后的“庆祝活动”

“Celebration Activities” after the Establishment of the So-called Reformed Government of the Republic of China

伪维新政府行政院院长梁鸿志在办公室

Liang Hongzhi, President of the Executive Yuan in His Office

伪维新政府的内阁会议

Cabinet Meeting of the So-called Reformed Government

伪维新政府官员在国民政府院内升旗

Officials of the so-called Reformed Government hoisted the flag in the courtyard of the Nationalist Government.

伪维新政府警卫大队在院内举行列队仪式

Guards of the so-called Reformed Government held a drill in the courtyard.

伪维新政府庆祝“维新初周”活动

The so-called Reformed Government held the celebration of “the First Week of Reform”.

1940 年 3 月 30 日，汪伪国民政府成立，日军仅同意在原国民政府设立伪立法院、考试院、监察院机关

Wang Jingwei's Puppet Government was established on 30 March 1940 and its Executive Yuan, Examination Yuan and Control Yuan used the former compound of the Nationalist Government as their offices.

国府东院沦为汪伪国民政府交通部和铁道部

The former east courtyard of the Nationalist Government housed the Ministries of Communications and Railways of Wang Jingwei's Puppet Government.

原国民政府参谋本部，沦为伪政权的绥靖部机关

The former office buildings of the HQs of General Staff of the Nationalist Government served as the “Ministry of Appeasement” of Wang Jingwei’s Puppet Government.

原国民政府参谋本部沦为汪伪政府军事参议院

Military Advisory Council under the Wang Jingwei’s Puppet Government settled in the former Headquarters of General Staff of the Nationalist Government.

七

国府还都　最后时光昙花现

VII. The Return of the Nationalist Government to Nanjing　A Period Lasted Briefly

1946年5月，国民政府“还都”南京，政治、军事、外事活动及各种会议频繁。同时，中共代表团由重庆移驻南京，继续进行国共谈判。

1947年11月、1948年4月，国民党单方面召开“制宪”国大和“行宪”国大，蒋介石、李宗仁分别当选“总统”“副总统”，国民政府改称总统府。1949年1月21日，蒋介石“下野”，李宗仁代理“总统”一职，并积极“谋和”，试图挽回局面。至4月23日，撤离南京。

In May 1946, the Nationalist Government returned to Nanjing. The activities of political, military and diplomatic affairs, as well as assemblies of the Nationalist Government were frequently held here. The Communist Delegation also removed from Chongqing to Nanjing at the same time. The Nationalist-Communist Peace Negotiations was continued.

The KMT held the Constitutional Convention in November 1947 and implemented the Constitution in April 1948. Chiang Kai-shek and Li Zongren were respectively elected as President and Vice President of the Republic of China. So that the Nationalist Government was then called the Presidential Government. On 21 January 1949, Chiang Kai-shek decided to “temporarily retire from office”, and Li Zongren took the post of Acting President. Li Zongren attempted to retrieve a defeat through peace negotiations. The Presidential Government withdrew from Nanjing by 23 April.

中華民國三十五年五月六日 中央日報

慶祝國民政府還都 昨隆重舉行大典 舉國同慶萬衆歡躍

蔣主席在陵前訓話

主席謁陵告文

國府禮堂茶會 主席招待外賓

有关国民政府“还都”及中共代表团参加相关活动的报道

Reports on the Nationalist Government's Return to the Capital and the Chinese Communist Party Delegation's Participation of Celebration Activities

1946 年 5 月，搭建在国民政府前的庆祝“还都”牌楼

Decorated archway was set up to celebrate the Nationalist Government's return to capital (Nanjing) in front of its gateway in May 1946.

1946 年"还都"时整修过的国民政府大门。门楼顶端已改为"山"形女儿墙，门上"国民政府"四字传为蒋介石所书

The Gate of the Nationalist Government was renovated in 1946 and the gate tower was changed into the appearance of "mountain". There were four Chinese characters "Guo Min Zheng Fu" (i.e. Nationalist Government) above the gate, which is said to be Chiang Kai-shek's calligraphy.

国民政府出入证及职员证

Gate Pass and Staff Card of the Nationalist Government

1946 年国民政府"还都"南京时，修葺一新的国府礼堂

The Grand Hall of the Nationalist Government was renovated after its return to Nanjing in 1946.

1946 年的“还都”广告

Advertisement for the Return to the Nanjing in 1946

1946 年 5 月，国民政府“还都”后组织的童子军游行

Boy Scouts held a celebration parade for the return to Nanjing of the Nationalist Government in May 1946.

国民政府“还都”后，国共和谈的重心由重庆移至南京。这是 1946 年 7 月《申报》关于周恩来与蒋介石在国民政府举行会谈的报道

A Report on the Talks Between Zhou Enlai and Chiang Kai-shek in the Nationalist Government was carried in “Shenbao” in July 1946.

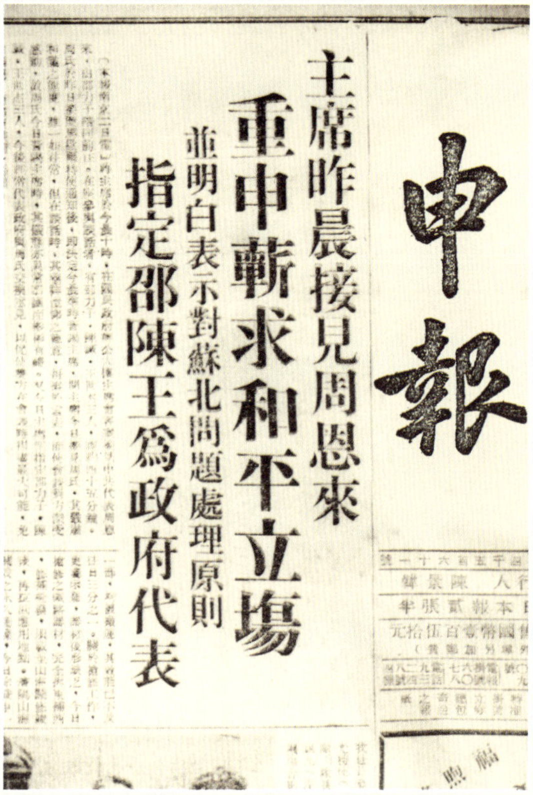

申報

主席昨晨接見周恩來

重申蘄求和平立場

並明白表示對蘇北問題處理原則

指定邵陳王爲政府代表

国共和谈的双方首席代表周恩来与张群

Zhou Enlai and Zhang Qun, Chief Representatives of the Nationalist-Communist Peace Delegations

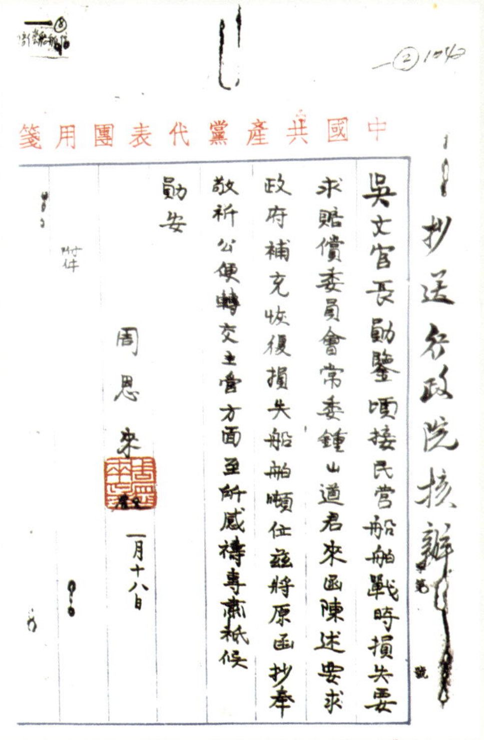

中國共產黨代表團用箋

抄送行政院核辦

吳文官長勛鑒：頃接民營船舶戰時損失要求賠償委員會常委鍾山道君來函陳述要求政府補充收復損失船舶噸位茲將原函抄奉敬祈公便轉交主管方面至所感禱專肅祇候

勛安

周恩來

一月十八日

附件

1947年1月18日，周恩来致国民政府文官长吴鼎昌函

Zhou Enlai's Message to Wu Dingchang, Chief of Civil Service of the Nationalist Government on 18 January 1947

中共代表团驻地——梅园新村30号，紧邻国民政府

30 Meiyuan Xincun, Nanjing, the Residence of the Communist Delegation, in the Close Neighbour of the Nationalist Government

“还都”后，国民政府在礼堂举行“总理纪念周”

“In Memory of Dr. Sun Yat-sen Weekly” was held in the Grand Hall of the Nationalist Government after its return.

1948 年元旦，国民政府举行新年团拜会

The Nationalist Government held an exchanging greetings with well-wishers on New Year’s Day on 1 January 1948.

1946年5月国民政府“还都”后，蒋介石在国民政府长廊检阅仪仗队

Chiang Kai-shek reviewed a guard of honour in May 1946 after the Nationalist Government's return to Nanjing.

1946年7月，宋子文、陈诚在国民政府检阅仪仗队

T.V. Soong and Chen Cheng reviewed a guard of honour in July 1946 after the Nationalist Government's return to Nanjing.

1947 年 4 月 23 日，国民政府改组会议在“子超楼”国务会议厅举行

Reorganization Conference of the Nationalist Government was held in the State Conference Hall of the “Zichao Building” on 23 April 1947.

“子超楼”国务会议厅（今摄）

State Conference Hall of the Presidential Palace (Picture taken in 2018)

1946 年 10 月 10 日，国民政府门前的庆祝活动

National Day Celebration in Front of the Gateway of the Nationalist Government on 10 October 1946

国民政府举行庆典活动

Celebration Activities Held by the Nationalist Government

外国来使的专车由宪兵警察护送进入国民政府

The special cars of diplomatic envoy entered the Presidential Palace escorted by military police.

1947年9月19日，蒋介石接见捷克大使

Chiang Kai-shek received the Czechoslovakian Ambassador to China on 19 September 1947.

1947年1月16日，波兰公使魏登涛在国民政府递交国书后步出礼堂

G. B. de Weydenthal, Polish Minister to China, stepped out of the Grand Hall of the Nationalist Government after presenting his credentials on 16 January 1947.

1947年5月13日上午10时，尼泊尔王国克利兴诺将军向国民政府呈递尼国王信函及最高勋章时，检阅仪仗队

A Nepalese General reviewed a guard of honour and conveyed the Nepalese King's letter and a Supreme Order of Nepal to the Nationalist Government at 10 a.m. on 13 May 1947.

蒋介石接见玻利维亚大使

Chiang Kai-shek received the Bolivian Ambassador to China.

1948 年，蒋介石与宋美龄在总统府会见美军顾问团团长巴大维

Chiang Kai-shek and Song Meiling (Mayling Soong) received the head of the American Military Advisory Commission in the Presidential Palace in 1948.

1948 年，蒋介石在会客室会见来访的外国军事要人

Chiang Kai-shek received foreign military VIPs in the reception room in 1948.

1948 年 3 月 5 日，蒋介石接见奥地利公使施德曼

Chiang Kai-shek received the Austrian Minister to China on 5 March 1948.

1948年6月1日，苏联驻华大使罗申（右二）在总统府递交国书

N. Roschin (second from right), Soviet Ambassador to China, presented his credentials in the Presidential Palace on 1 June 1948.

1948 年，新到任的土耳其驻华大使在总统府呈递到任国书

The new Turkish Ambassador to China presented his credentials in the Presidential Palace in 1948.

缅甸大使密登在总统府呈递国书

The Burmese Ambassador Presenting His Credentials in the Presidential Palace

1948 年，外交部部长王世杰会见美国大使司徒雷登等

Wang Shijie, Minister of Foreign Affairs, received J. L. Stuart, American Ambassador to China in 1948.

总统府车队

Motor cars of the Presidential Palace

1948年10月10日，蒋介石在总统府举行的庆典仪式上讲话

Chiang Kai-shek spoke at the National Day Celebration in the Presidential Palace on 10 October 1948.

1948年10月10日，纪念“双十节”时的总统府大门

The Gate of the Presidential Palace on 10 October 1948

1947 年 1 月 2 日，金陵大学等高校学生抗暴游行，向国民政府递交请愿书

Students of the Nanking University and other colleges held a demonstration to protest the outrages of military police and presented a petition to the Nationalist Government on 2 January 1947.

前往国民政府游行示威的学生途经国民大会堂

Demonstrational students went to the Nationalist Government by way of the People's Hall.

1947年5月20日，前往国民政府游行示威的学生在国府路与军警对峙六小时

Demonstrational students confronted with the military police for six hours in the street of the Nationalist Government on 20 May 1947.

南京高校学生在国民政府前抗议游行

Students from Nanjing universities and colleges held a protest march in front of the Nationalist Government.

1947 年 11 月“制宪”国大期间，国民政府“五院”院长的合影

Presidents of “Five-Yuan” of the Nationalist Government had a photo taken during the Constitutional Convention in November 1947.

1948 年 4 月，“行宪”国大在国民政府西侧的国民大会堂举行。蒋介石、李宗仁分别当选“总统”“副总统”

Implementing the Constitution convention was held in the People's Hall. Chiang Kai-shek and Li Zongren were respectively elected as President and Vice President in April 1948.

1948年4月“行宪”国大期间，蒋介石等在礼堂

Chiang Kai-shek et al. in the Grand Hall during the National Congress to implement the Constitution in April 1948

1948年5月“行宪”国大后，蒋介石在总统府办公室批阅公文

Chiang Kai-shek read over official papers in his office of the Presidential Government in May 1948.

1948年5月20日，蒋介石当选“总统”后与夫人宋美龄

President Chiang Kai-shek posed with his wife Song Meiling on 20 May 1948.

“副总统”李宗仁与夫人郭德洁

Vice President Posing with His Wife Guo Dejie

“总统”“副总统”就职仪式结束后，蒋介石、宋美龄、李宗仁、郭德洁在礼堂休息室交谈

President Chiang Kai-shek and his wife Song Meiling, and Vice President Li Zongren and his wife Guo Dejie talked with each other after the inauguration on 20 May 1948.

1948 年 5 月 20 日“总统”就职仪式后，当局在总统府门前举行庆祝活动

A celebration was held in front of the gateway of the Presidential Palace after the inaugural ceremony of the President and Vice President on 20 May 1948.

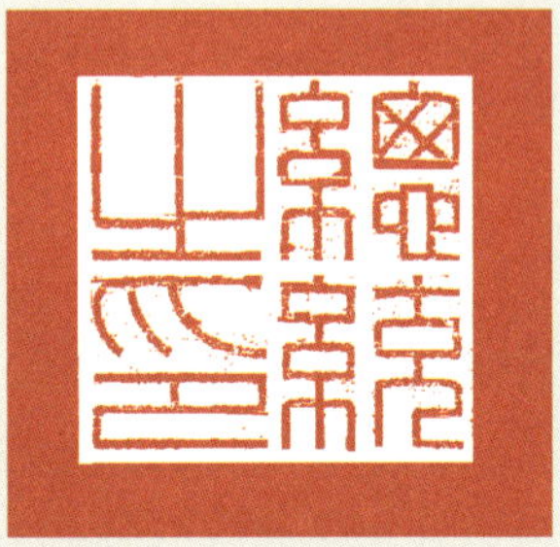

“总统之印”印文

The Seal of the President

1948年5月20日“总统”“副总统”就职仪式结束后，蒋介石、李宗仁与国民党党政军要人在“子超楼”前合影。这是国民党在大陆的最后一张“全家福”

President Chiang Kai-shek and Vice President Li Zongren posed for a group photo with important political and military officials after the inauguration in front of "Zichao Building" on 20 May 1948.

“行宪”国大后的总统府大门

The Gate of the Presidential Palace

1949年1月21日，蒋介石“下野”，李宗仁代理“总统”一职

On 21 January 1949, Chiang Kai-shek decided to “temporarily retire from office”, and Li Zongren took the office of Acting President.

1949年1月，总统府秘书长吴鼎昌辞职，与同仁在“子超楼”前合影

Wu Dingchang, Secretary-General of the Presidential Government, posed for a photo with his colleagues in front of “Zichao Building” in January 1949.

1949年1月，“代总统”李宗仁在总统府会见美国大使司徒雷登

Acting President Li Zongren received J. L. Stuart, Ambassador of the U. S., in the Presidential Palace in January 1949.

“代总统”李宗仁在总统府会见外宾

Acting President Li Zongren received foreign guests in the Presidential Palace.

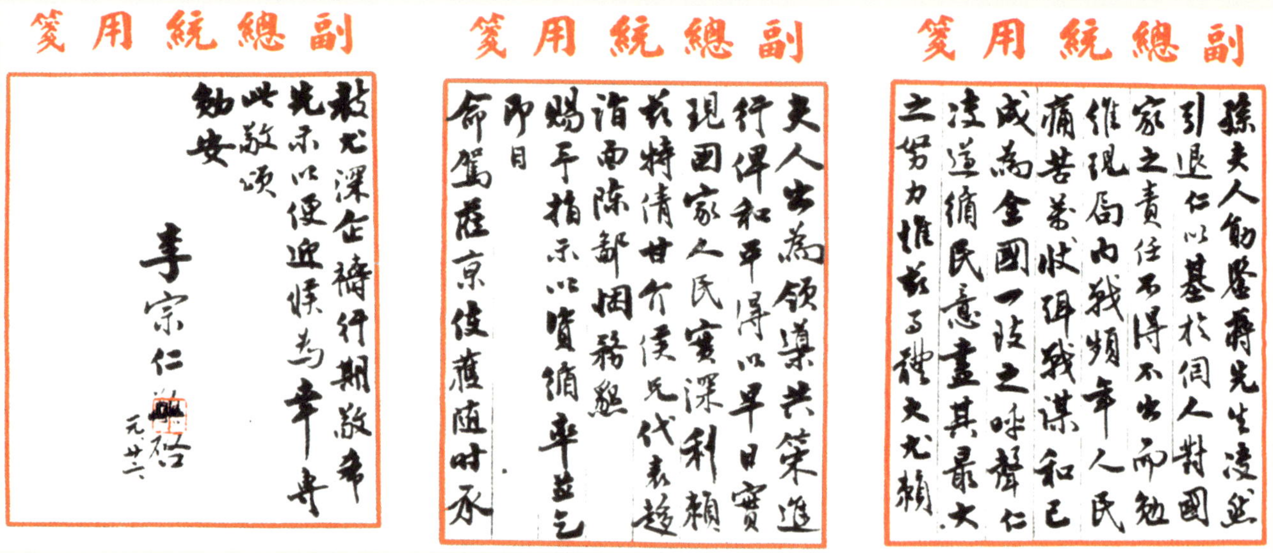

副總統用箋

孫夫人勛鑒：蔣先生既已引退，仁以基於個人對國家之責任，不得不出而勉維現局。內戰頻年，人民痛苦萬狀，弭戰謀和，已成為全國一致之呼聲。仁遵循民意，盡其最大之努力，惟茲事體大，尤賴

副總統用箋

夫人出為領導，共策進行，俾和平得以早日實現，國家人民實深利賴。茲特請甘介侯先生代表趨謁，面陳鄙悃，務懇賜予指示，以資循率，並乞即日命駕蒞京，俾獲隨時承

副總統用箋

教，尤深企禱，佇期敬希先示，以便迎候為幸。專此敬頌
勛安
李宗仁敬啓
元廿六

1949 年 1 月 22 日，“代总统”李宗仁致函宋庆龄，请其赴南京“出为领导，共策进行”

Li Zongren’s message to Song Qingling invited her to come to Nanjing to help him administer the country on 22 January 1949.

李宗仁在总统府接见邵力子等和平人士

Li Zongren received Shao Lizi and other pacifists in the Presidential Palace.

1949年4月1日，南京大专院校师生在总统府门前举行要求“国民党接受中共中央的八项和平条件，实现真正和平”的示威游行

Teachers and students from Nanjing universities and colleges held a demonstration opposing the civil war in front of the gate of the Presidential Palace on 1 April 1949.

1949年4月1日，游行示威的学生在总统府前遭殴打

On 1 April 1949, students from universities and colleges participated in the demonstration was hit in front of the Presidential Palace.

国共和谈（油画）

The Nationalist–Communist Peace Negotiations (Oil Painting)

八

煦园曙光　总统府进入新纪元

VIII. Dawn of the Xu Garden　The Presidential Palace Entering a New Era

钟山风雨起苍黄，百万雄师过大江。1949年4月23日，南京解放。24日凌晨，中国人民解放军第三野战军35军104师312团3营官兵占领总统府。渡江战役总前委成员相继进入总统府。国民党在中国大陆的统治宣告终结。从此，总统府跨入新纪元。

Over Zhongshan swept a storm, head long, Our mighty army has crossed the great river a million strong. On 23 April 1949, the Chinese People's Liberation Army liberated Nanjing. An advance force occupied the Presidential Palace in the small hours of 24 April. It indicated the ending of the Kuomintang's rule in the mainland. From that day the Presidential Palace has strode into a new era.

1949 年 4 月 21 日，人民解放军发起渡江作战。长江江面，千舟竞发，兵锋直指江南，国民党军江防顷刻土崩瓦解

The PLA fought across the Yangtze River on 21 April 1949 and the river defense of the KMT troops was disintegrated.

解放军战士登上长江南岸

The PLA soldiers climbed up to the south dyke of the Yangtze River.

人民解放军进入南京挹江门，受到市民热烈欢迎

The PLA soldiers entered in the Yijiang Gate of Nanjing and were warmly welcomed by citizens of Nanjing.

人民解放军坦克部队通过市中心新街口，向总统府进发

The tank forces of the PLA passing the center of Nanjing city started for the Presidential Palace.

1949年4月23日，南京解放。24日凌晨，解放军进入总统府，推开总统府大门

Nanjing was liberated on 23 April 1949. In the small hours of April 24, the People's Liberation Army pushed open the gate of the Presidential Palace and occupied it.

解放军战士冲入总统府

Officers and men of the PLA dashed into the Presidential Palace.

蒋介石的“总统”办公室

President Chiang Kai-shek's Office

“总统”办公室的台历定格在 4 月 23 日

Calendar on Chiang Kai-shek's Desk Showing the Date of 23 April 1949

办公桌上的《曾文正公全集》

“Complete Works of Zeng Guofan” on Chiang Kai-shek's Official Table

“总统办公室”木牌

Board with “the President's Office”

办公桌上的小座钟

Clock on Chiang Kai-shek's Official Table

蒋介石的签章印

Seal of “Jiang Zhongzheng” on Chiang Kai-shek's Desk

（部分原件藏中国国家博物馆）

总统府办公室内凌乱不堪

In a Fearful Mess of All Offices in the Presidential Palace

总统府标识牌

Signboard in the Presidential Palace

总统府案卷

Files of the Presidential Government

国民政府在景德镇定制的金地万花粉彩瓷餐具，又称“国府御瓷”。在“子超楼”地下室发现

A series of the Nationalist Government porcelain was produced in the Jingdezhen Porcelain Factory in the 1930s.

（原件藏南京市博物馆）

1949 年 4 月 24 日凌晨 2 时许，中国人民解放军第三野战军 35 军 104 师 312 团 3 营特务连官兵率先占领总统府。这帧照片，成为中国近代史上的经典之作

An advance force occupied the Presidential Palace at 2 a.m. of 24 April 1949.

解放军占领总统府后，降下了青天白日旗

After the PLA's occupation of the Presidential Palace, the army men tore down the blue sky and white sun flag.

毛泽东在北平香山双清别墅阅读“南京解放”号外

Mao Zedong Reading the Extra of a Newspaper Reporting on the Liberation of Nanjing in His Beiping Residence

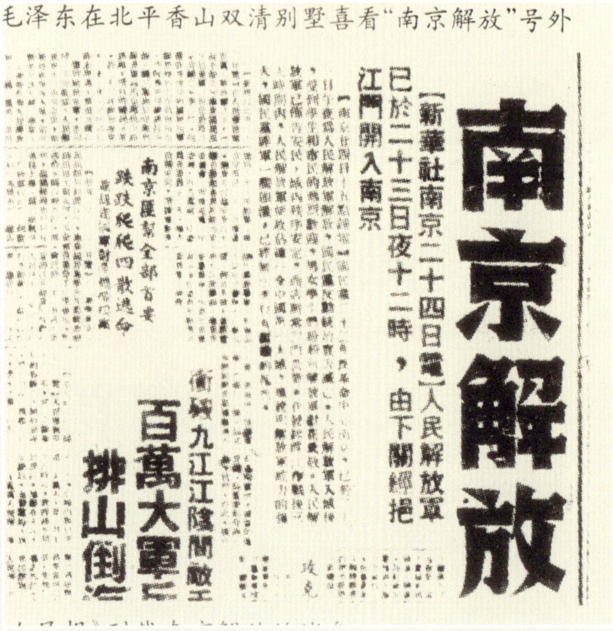

毛泽东在北平香山双清别墅喜看“南京解放”号外

南京解放

〔新華社南京二十四日電〕人民解放軍已於二十三日夜十二時，由下關繹挹江門開入南京

南京匪幫全部首要
狼狽紛紛四散逃命

衝破九江江陰間敵
百萬大軍
排山倒

南京解放的报道

News Reporting on the Liberation of Nanjing

1949 年 4 月 27 日，南京各界在总统府门前欢庆解放

People from all walks of life celebrated the liberation of Nanjing in front of the gateway of the Presidential Palace on 27 April 1949.

解放军官兵在总统府大院中休整

Officers and Men of the PLA Having a Rest in the Courtyard of the Presidential Palace

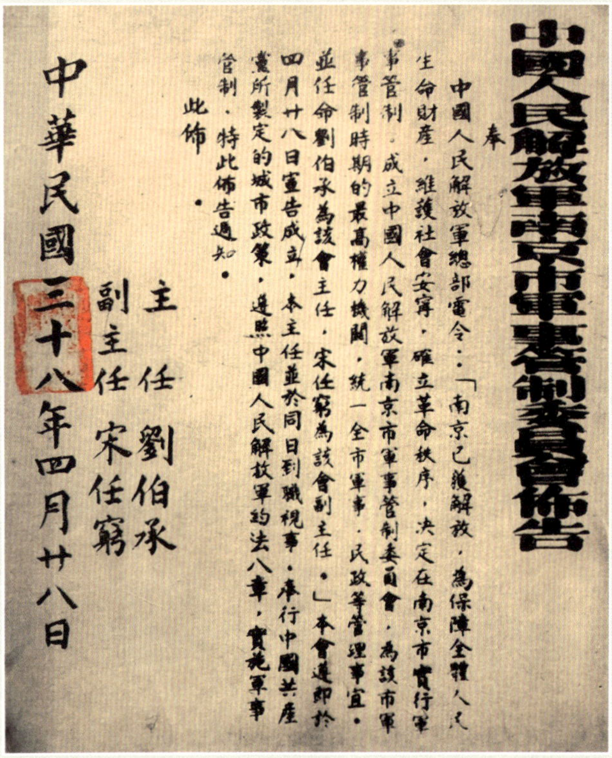

中國人民解放軍南京市軍事管制委員會佈告

奉

中國人民解放軍總部電令：「南京已獲解放，為保障全體人民生命財產，維護社會安寧，確立革命秩序，決定在南京市實行軍事管制，成立中國人民解放軍南京市軍事管制委員會，為該市軍事管制時期的最高權力機關，統一全市軍事、民政等管理事宜，並任命劉伯承為該會主任，宋任窮為該會副主任。」本會遵即於四月廿八日宣告成立，本主任並於同日到職視事，奉行中國共產黨所製定的城市政策，遵照中國人民解放軍約法八章，實施軍事管制，特此佈告週知。

此佈

主任 劉伯承

副主任 宋任窮

中華民國三十八年四月廿八日

南京市军管会布告

Notice of the Nanjing Military Control Commission

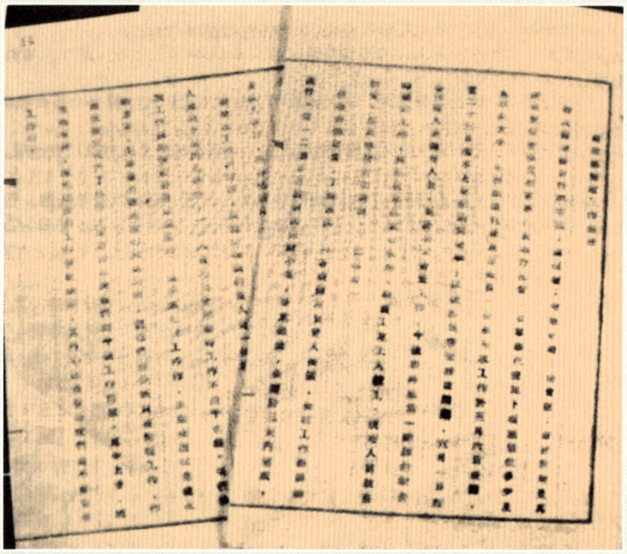

南京市军管会接管总统府报告

Report on the Taking over the Presidential Palace by the Nanjing Military Control Commission

南京解放时，渡江战役总前委成员相继进入总统府，部署接管总统府及保护文物工作，接见国民党起义将领和爱国人士，筹划南下的军事行动等

After the libration of Nanjing, members of the Front Line Command Committee of the PLA River–crossing Campaign successively entered the Presidential Palace to take over the Presidential Palace and the protection of cultural relics; to meet KMT insurgent generals and patriots; and planning military operations south, etc.

渡江战役总前委书记、第二野战军政委邓小平

Deng Xiaoping, Secretary of the Front Line Command Committee of the PLA River-crossing Campaign, Political Commissar of the Second Field Army entered the Presidential Palace on 27 April 1949.

渡江战役总前委成员、第二野战军司令员刘伯承。后任南京市军管会主任，首任南京市长

Liu Bocheng, Member of the Front Line Command Committee of the PLA River-crossing Campaign, Commander of the Second Field Army entered the Presidential Palace on 29 April 1949.

渡江战役总前委成员、第三野战军司令员陈毅

Chen Yi, Member of the Front Line Command Committee of the PLA River-crossing Campaign, Commander of the Third Field Army entered the Presidential Palace on 27 April 1949.

渡江战役总前委成员、第三野战军副司令员粟裕。接任南京市军管会主任，南京市第一届各界人民代表会议主席

Su Yu, Member of the Front Line Command Committee of the PLA River-crossing Campaign, Deputy Commander of the Third Field Army entered the Presidential Palace on 26 April 1949.

渡江战役总前委成员、第三野战军副政委谭震林

Tan Zhenlin, Member of the Front Line Command Committee of the PLA River-crossing Campaign, Deputy Political Commissar of the Third Field Army

中国人民解放军第二野战军司令员、南京市军事管制委员会主任、南京市市长刘伯承，在总统府接见率领国民党海军第二舰队起义的舰队司令林遵少将等人

Liu Bocheng, Director of the Nanjing Military Control Commission received Lin Zun, Commander of the surrendered Second Fleet of the KMT Navy.

刘伯承与林遵在总统府

Liu Bocheng with Lin Zun in the Presidential Palace

国民党海军第二舰队司令林遵

Lin Zun, Commander of the Second Fleet of the Kuomintang Navy

解放军战士在总统府长廊站岗

Soldiers of the PLA were on sentry duty along the long veranda of the Presidential Palace.

南京解放时的总统府国务会议厅

State Conference Hall of the Presidential Government during the Liberation of Nanjing

南京解放后，人民海军列队进入总统府参观

Officers and Men of the People's Navy Visiting the Presidential Palace after the Liberation of Nanjing

煦园曙光（油画）

Dawn in the Xu Garden (Oil Painting, by Chen Jian)

总统府历史沿革表

Table of Historical Change of the Presidential Palace

（1368—1949年）

明 朝			
归德侯府	归德侯（汉王）	陈 理	1368
黔宁王府	黔宁王	沐 英	1377
汉王府	汉 王	朱高煦（明成祖朱棣次子）	1404
清 朝			
两江总督署（江南总督署）	总 督	郎廷佐 尹继善等	1665—1853
太平天国天朝宫殿（天王府）	天 王	洪秀全	1853—1864
两江总督署	总 督	曾国藩 张人骏等	1864—1911.12
林都督行辕	都 督	林述庆	1911.12
江浙联军总司令部	总司令	徐绍桢	1911.12
中华民国临时政府			
总统府	临时大总统	孙中山	1912.1.1—1912.4.1
中华民国政府（北洋）			
南京留守府	留 守	黄 兴	1912.4.1—1912.5.31
江苏都督府	都 督	程德全	1912.6.14—1913.7.16
江苏都督府	都督（代）	庄蕴宽	1913
江苏讨袁军总司令部	司 令	黄 兴	1913.7.15—1913.7.28
江苏都督府	都督（代）	章 梓	1913.7

江苏讨袁军总司令部	司　令	何海鸣	1913.8.8—1913.9.1
江苏都督府	都　督	张　勋	1913.9.1—1913.9.12
江苏都督府	都　督	冯国璋	1913.12—1914.6
江苏将军府	将　军	冯国璋	1914.6—1916.7
江苏督军署	督　军	冯国璋	1916.7—1917.8
中华民国副总统府	副总统	冯国璋	1916.10—1917.8
江苏督军署	督军（代）	齐耀琳	1917.7
江苏督军署	督　军	李　纯	1917.8—1920.10.12
江苏督军署	督　军	齐燮元	1920.10.15—1924.12.11
江苏督军署（督办公署）	督办（代）	韩国钧	1924.12—1925.1
江苏督办公署（宣抚使署）	督办（宣抚使）	卢永祥	1925.1—1925.8
江苏督办公署	督　办	郑　谦	1925.8
江苏督办公署	督　办	杨宇霆	1925.8—1925.11
江苏督办公署（后称五省联军总司令部）	督办（总司令）	孙传芳	1925.11.25—1927.3.24
直鲁联军联合办事处	主　任	张宗昌	1927.3.19—1927.3.24
中华民国国民政府			
国民革命军总司令部（北伐军总司令部）	总司令	蒋介石	1927.3
国民政府军事委员会	主席团委员	蒋介石 李宗仁等	1927.4
国民政府	常务委员	胡汉民　古应芬 伍朝枢　张人杰	1927.4.18—1927.9.17
国民政府	常务委员	汪兆铭　谭延闿 胡汉民　蔡元培 李烈钧	1927.9.17—1928.1

国民政府	常务委员	汪兆铭 谭延闿 胡汉民 蔡元培 李烈钧 于右任 蒋介石 孙 科 林 森	1928.1—1928.2
国民政府	主 席	谭延闿	1928.2—1928.10
国民政府	主 席	蒋介石	1928.10—1931.12.15
国民政府	主席（代）	林 森	1931.12.15
国民政府	主 席	林 森	1932.1.1—1932.1.31
国民政府（洛阳）	主 席	林 森	1932.1.31—1932.12.1
国民政府	主 席	林 森	1932.12.1—1937.11
国民政府（重庆）	主 席	林 森	1937.11—1943.8
国民政府（重庆）	主 席	蒋介石	1943.8—1946.5
南京沦陷（日伪政权）			
日军第十六师团部（中岛部队）	师团长	中岛今朝吾	1937.12—1938.3
伪维新政府行政院	院 长	梁鸿志	1938.3.28—1940.3.30
汪伪政府监察院	院 长	梁鸿志	1940.3.30—1944.11
汪伪政府监察院	院 长	顾忠琛	1944.11—1945.8
汪伪政府立法院	院 长	陈公博	1940.3.30—1944.11
汪伪政府立法院	院 长	梁鸿志	1944.11—1945.8
汪伪政府考试院	院 长	王揖唐	1940.3.30—1942.3
汪伪政府考试院	院 长	江亢虎	1942.3—1945.8
中华民国国民政府 总统府			
国民政府	主 席	蒋介石	1946.5—1948.4.18
总统府	总 统	蒋介石	1948.4.19—1949.1.21
总统府	代总统	李宗仁	1949.1.21—1949.4.23

后　记

一位哲人说："一座总统府，就是一部中国近代史。"正因如此，总统府备受海内外的广泛关注。

《百年总统府》成书历经数十年的积累和考证研究。图书编写体例，以年代为纲，以人物、事件、建筑为目。收入的相关照片，有的是首次披露，并适当插配一些今摄彩图进行对比。19世纪中叶，摄影技术尚未完备，故太平天国部分未能收入相关照片。

在本书编撰过程中，有关图书馆、档案馆、党史办、地方志、博物馆、纪念馆、大专院校、出版机构等单位给予了大力支持和帮助；朱明镜、邹建东、韩品峥、吴志明等老同志，蔡鸿源、党德信、苏炳根、高晓星等专家学者，多年来在史料提供及考证研究方面，一直给予关心和指导；苏正茂、任凤鸣、于川、夏蓓、时平、袁斌、沈岚、巫勇、武学沪等在本书编辑工作中也给予了诸多帮助。在本书付梓之际，在此表示诚挚的谢意！

Postscript

A philosopher said: "a presidential palace, is a modern history of China." Because of this, the Presidential Palace has been widely concerned at home and abroad.

The compilation of this book took several years.The compilation style of this book takes the time as the outline, takes the person, the event, the architecture as the details. Some historical data are disclosed for the first time, and some colour pictures taken today are appropriately inserted for comparison. In the middle of the 19th century, photography technology was not complete, so part of the Taiping Heavenly Kingdom was not included in the relevant photos.

In the process of compiling this book, libraries, archives, party history offices, local chronicles, museums, memorial halls, colleges and universities, publishing institutions and other units at all levels have given strong support and assistance. Zhu Mingjing, Zou Jiandong, Han Pinzheng,Wu Zhiming, Cai Hongyuan, Dang Dexin, Su Binggen, Gao Xiaoxing and other veteran comrades, experts and scholars have been giving care and guidance for many years. Su Zhengmao, Ren Fengming, Yu Chuan, Xia Bei, Shi Ping, Yuan Bin, Shen Lan,Wu Yong, Wu Xuehu and others have also given support and help in the editing of this book. On the occasion of the publication of this book, we would like to express our sincere thanks!

图书在版编目（CIP）数据

百年总统府 / 刘晓宁, 郭必强主编. -- 南京 : 南京出版社, 2019.7

ISBN 978-7-5533-2514-9

Ⅰ. ①百… Ⅱ. ①刘… ②郭… Ⅲ. ①国民政府－纪念地－史料－南京 Ⅳ. ①K878.23

中国版本图书馆CIP数据核字（2019）第028122号

书　　名 百年总统府
主　　编 刘晓宁　郭必强
出版发行 南京出版传媒集团
南 京 出 版 社

社址　南京市太平门街53号　　邮编　210016
网址　http://www.njcbs.cn　　电子信箱　njcbs1988@163.com
天猫1店　https://njcbcmjtts.tmall.com/　　天猫2店　https://nanjingchubanshets.tmall.com/
联系电话　025-83283893、83283864（营销）　025-83112257（编务）

出 版 人 项晓宁
出 品 人 卢海鸣
责任编辑 徐　智
装帧设计 王　俊
责任印制 杨福彬

排　　版 南京新华丰制版有限公司
印　　刷 南京艺中印务有限公司
开　　本 889毫米×1194毫米　1/16
印　　张 14.25
字　　数 274千
版　　次 2019年7月第1版
印　　次 2019年7月第1次印刷
书　　号 ISBN 978-7-5533-2514-9
定　　价 100.00元

天猫1店　天猫2店